Connected Mathematics 2™

Bits and Pieces I

Understanding Fractions, Decimals, and Percents

Glenda Lappan

James T. Fey

William M. Fitzgerald

Susan N. Friel

Elizabeth Difanis Phillips

PEARSON

Boston, Massachusetts · Glenview, Illinois · Shoreview, Minnesota · Upper Saddle River, New Jersey

Connected Mathematics™ was developed at Michigan State University with financial support from the Michigan State University Office of the Provost, Computing and Technology, and the College of Natural Science.

This material is based upon work supported by the National Science Foundation under Grant No. MDR 9150217 and Grant No. ESI 9986372. Opinions expressed are those of the authors and not necessarily those of the Foundation.

The Michigan State University authors and administration have agreed that all MSU royalties arising from this publication will be devoted to purposes supported by the MSU Mathematics Education Enrichment Fund.

13-digit ISBN 978-0-13-366130-9
10-digit ISBN 0-13-366130-X
1 2 3 4 5 6 7 8 9 10   11 10 09 08

Authors of Connected Mathematics

(from left to right) Glenda Lappan, Betty Phillips, Susan Friel, Bill Fitzgerald, Jim Fey

Glenda Lappan is a University Distinguished Professor in the Department of Mathematics at Michigan State University. Her research and development interests are in the connected areas of students' learning of mathematics and mathematics teachers' professional growth and change related to the development and enactment of K–12 curriculum materials.

James T. Fey is a Professor of Curriculum and Instruction and Mathematics at the University of Maryland. His consistent professional interest has been development and research focused on curriculum materials that engage middle and high school students in problem-based collaborative investigations of mathematical ideas and their applications.

William M. Fitzgerald (*Deceased*) was a Professor in the Department of Mathematics at Michigan State University. His early research was on the use of concrete materials in supporting student learning and led to the development of teaching materials for laboratory environments. Later he helped develop a teaching model to support student experimentation with mathematics.

Susan N. Friel is a Professor of Mathematics Education in the School of Education at the University of North Carolina at Chapel Hill. Her research interests focus on statistics education for middle-grade students and, more broadly, on teachers' professional development and growth in teaching mathematics K–8.

Elizabeth Difanis Phillips is a Senior Academic Specialist in the Mathematics Department of Michigan State University. She is interested in teaching and learning mathematics for both teachers and students. These interests have led to curriculum and professional development projects at the middle school and high school levels, as well as projects related to the teaching and learning of algebra across the grades.

Field Test Sites for CMP2

During the development of the revised edition of *Connected Mathematics* (CMP2), more than 100 classroom teachers have field-tested materials at 49 school sites in 12 states and the District of Columbia. This classroom testing occurred over three academic years (2001 through 2004), allowing careful study of the effectiveness of each of the 24 units that comprise the program. A special thanks to the students and teachers at these pilot schools.

Arkansas
Magnolia Public Schools
Kittena Bell*, Judith Trowell*; *Central Elementary School:* Maxine Broom, Betty Eddy, Tiffany Fallin, Bonnie Flurry, Carolyn Monk, Elizabeth Tye; *Magnolia Junior High School:* Monique Bryan, Ginger Cook, David Graham, Shelby Lamkin

Colorado
Boulder Public Schools
Nevin Platt Middle School: Judith Koenig

St. Vrain Valley School District, Longmont
Westview Middle School: Colleen Beyer, Kitty Canupp, Ellie Decker*, Peggy McCarthy, Tanya deNobrega, Cindy Payne, Ericka Pilon, Andrew Roberts

District of Columbia
Capitol Hill Day School: Ann Lawrence

Georgia
University of Georgia, Athens
Brad Findell

Madison Public Schools
Morgan County Middle School: Renee Burgdorf, Lynn Harris, Nancy Kurtz, Carolyn Stewart

Maine
Falmouth Public Schools
Falmouth Middle School: Donna Erikson, Joyce Hebert, Paula Hodgkins, Rick Hogan, David Legere, Cynthia Martin, Barbara Stiles, Shawn Towle*

Michigan
Portland Public Schools
Portland Middle School: Mark Braun, Holly DeRosia, Kathy Dole*, Angie Foote, Teri Keusch, Tammi Wardwell

Traverse City Area Public Schools
Bertha Vos Elementary: Kristin Sak; *Central Grade School:* Michelle Clark; Jody Meyers; *Eastern Elementary:* Karrie Tufts; *Interlochen Elementary:* Mary McGee-Cullen; *Long Lake Elementary:* Julie Faulkner*, Charlie Maxbauer, Katherine Sleder; *Norris Elementary:* Hope Slanaker; *Oak Park Elementary:* Jessica Steed; *Traverse Heights Elementary:* Jennifer Wolfert; *Westwoods Elementary:* Nancy Conn; *Old Mission Peninsula School:* Deb Larimer; *Traverse City East Junior High:* Ivanka Berkshire, Ruthanne Kladder, Jan Palkowski, Jane Peterson, Mary Beth Schmitt; *Traverse City West Junior High:* Dan Fouch*, Ray Fouch

Sturgis Public Schools
Sturgis Middle School: Ellen Eisele

Minnesota
Burnsville School District 191
Hidden Valley Elementary: Stephanie Cin, Jane McDevitt

Hopkins School District 270
Alice Smith Elementary: Sandra Cowing, Kathleen Gustafson, Martha Mason, Scott Stillman; *Eisenhower Elementary:* Chad Bellig, Patrick Berger, Nancy Glades, Kye Johnson, Shane Wasserman, Victoria Wilson; *Gatewood Elementary:* Sarah Ham, Julie Kloos, Janine Pung, Larry Wade; *Glen Lake Elementary:* Jacqueline Cramer, Kathy Hering, Cecelia Morris, Robb Trenda; *Katherine Curren Elementary:* Diane Bancroft, Sue DeWit, John Wilson; *L. H. Tanglen Elementary:* Kevin Athmann, Lisa Becker, Mary LaBelle, Kathy Rezac, Roberta Severson; *Meadowbrook Elementary:* Jan Gauger, Hildy Shank, Jessica Zimmerman; *North Junior High:* Laurel Hahn, Kristin Lee, Jodi Markuson, Bruce Mestemacher, Laurel Miller, Bonnie Rinker, Jeannine Salzer, Sarah Shafer, Cam Stottler; *West Junior High:* Alicia Beebe, Kristie Earl, Nobu Fujii, Pam Georgetti, Susan Gilbert, Regina Nelson Johnson, Debra Lindstrom, Michele Luke*, Jon Sorenson

Minneapolis School District 1
Ann Sullivan K-8 School: Bronwyn Collins; Anne Bartel* (Curriculum and Instruction Office)

Wayzata School District 284
Central Middle School: Sarajane Myers, Dan Nielsen, Tanya Ravenholdt

White Bear Lake School District 624
Central Middle School: Amy Jorgenson, Michelle Reich, Brenda Sammon

New York
New York City Public Schools
IS 89: Yelena Aynbinder, Chi-Man Ng, Nina Rapaport, Joel Spengler, Phyllis Tam*, Brent Wyso; *Wagner Middle School:* Jason Appel, Intissar Fernandez, Yee Gee Get, Richard Goldstein, Irving Marcus, Sue Norton, Bernadita Owens, Jennifer Rehn*, Kevin Yuhas

---

* indicates a Field Test Site Coordinator

Ohio
Talawanda School District, Oxford
Talawanda Middle School: Teresa Abrams, Larry Brock, Heather Brosey, Julie Churchman, Monna Even, Karen Fitch, Bob George, Amanda Klee, Pat Meade, Sandy Montgomery, Barbara Sherman, Lauren Steidl

Miami University
Jeffrey Wanko*

Springfield Public Schools
Rockway School: Jim Mamer

Pennsylvania
Pittsburgh Public Schools
Kenneth Labuskes, Marianne O'Connor, Mary Lynn Raith*; *Arthur J. Rooney Middle School:* David Hairston, Stamatina Mousetis, Alfredo Zangaro; *Frick International Studies Academy:* Suzanne Berry, Janet Falkowski, Constance Finseth, Romika Hodge, Frank Machi; *Reizenstein Middle School:* Jeff Baldwin, James Brautigam, Lorena Burnett, Glen Cobbett, Michael Jordan, Margaret Lazur, Melissa Munnell, Holly Neely, Ingrid Reed, Dennis Reft

Texas
Austin Independent School District
Bedichek Middle School: Lisa Brown, Jennifer Glasscock, Vicki Massey

El Paso Independent School District
Cordova Middle School: Armando Aguirre, Anneliesa Durkes, Sylvia Guzman, Pat Holguin*, William Holguin, Nancy Nava, Laura Orozco, Michelle Peña, Roberta Rosen, Patsy Smith, Jeremy Wolf

Plano Independent School District
Patt Henry, James Wohlgehagen*; *Frankford Middle School:* Mandy Baker, Cheryl Butsch, Amy Dudley, Betsy Eshelman, Janet Greene, Cort Haynes, Kathy Letchworth, Kay Marshall, Kelly McCants, Amy Reck, Judy Scott, Syndy Snyder, Lisa Wang; *Wilson Middle School:* Darcie Bane, Amanda Bedenko, Whitney Evans, Tonelli Hatley, Sarah (Becky) Higgs, Kelly Johnston, Rebecca McElligott, Kay Neuse, Cheri Slocum, Kelli Straight

Washington
Evergreen School District
Shahala Middle School: Nicole Abrahamsen, Terry Coon*, Carey Doyle, Sheryl Drechsler, George Gemma, Gina Helland, Amy Hilario, Darla Lidyard, Sean McCarthy, Tilly Meyer, Willow Neuwelt, Todd Parsons, Brian Pederson, Stan Posey, Shawn Scott, Craig Sjoberg, Lynette Sundstrom, Charles Switzer, Luke Youngblood

Wisconsin
Beaver Dam Unified School District
Beaver Dam Middle School: Jim Braemer, Jeanne Frick, Jessica Greatens, Barbara Link, Dennis McCormick, Karen Michels, Nancy Nichols*, Nancy Palm, Shelly Stelsel, Susan Wiggins

---

* indicates a Field Test Site Coordinator

Reviews of CMP to Guide Development of CMP2

Before writing for CMP2 began or field tests were conducted, the first edition of *Connected Mathematics* was submitted to the mathematics faculties of school districts from many parts of the country and to 80 individual reviewers for extensive comments.

School District Survey Reviews of CMP

Arizona
Madison School District #38 (Phoenix)

Arkansas
Cabot School District, Little Rock School District, Magnolia School District

California
Los Angeles Unified School District

Colorado
St. Vrain Valley School District (Longmont)

Florida
Leon County Schools (Tallahassee)

Illinois
School District #21 (Wheeling)

Indiana
Joseph L. Block Junior High (East Chicago)

Kentucky
Fayette County Public Schools (Lexington)

Maine
Selection of Schools

Massachusetts
Selection of Schools

Michigan
Sparta Area Schools

Minnesota
Hopkins School District

Texas
Austin Independent School District, The El Paso Collaborative for Academic Excellence, Plano Independent School District

Wisconsin
Platteville Middle School

Individual Reviewers of CMP

Arkansas

Deborah Cramer; Robby Frizzell *(Taylor)*; Lowell Lynde *(University of Arkansas, Monticello)*; Leigh Manzer *(Norfork)*; Lynne Roberts *(Emerson High School, Emerson)*; Tony Timms *(Cabot Public Schools)*; Judith Trowell *(Arkansas Department of Higher Education)*

California

José Alcantar *(Gilroy)*; Eugenie Belcher *(Gilroy)*; Marian Pasternack *(Lowman M. S. T. Center, North Hollywood)*; Susana Pezoa *(San Jose)*; Todd Rabusin *(Hollister)*; Margaret Siegfried *(Ocala Middle School, San Jose)*; Polly Underwood *(Ocala Middle School, San Jose)*

Colorado

Janeane Golliher *(St. Vrain Valley School District, Longmont)*; Judith Koenig *(Nevin Platt Middle School, Boulder)*

Florida

Paige Loggins *(Swift Creek Middle School, Tallahassee)*

Illinois

Jan Robinson *(School District #21, Wheeling)*

Indiana

Frances Jackson *(Joseph L. Block Junior High, East Chicago)*

Kentucky

Natalee Feese *(Fayette County Public Schools, Lexington)*

Maine

Betsy Berry *(Maine Math & Science Alliance, Augusta)*

Maryland

Joseph Gagnon *(University of Maryland, College Park)*; Paula Maccini *(University of Maryland, College Park)*

Massachusetts

George Cobb *(Mt. Holyoke College, South Hadley)*; Cliff Kanold *(University of Massachusetts, Amherst)*

Michigan

Mary Bouck *(Farwell Area Schools)*; Carol Dorer *(Slauson Middle School, Ann Arbor)*; Carrie Heaney *(Forsythe Middle School, Ann Arbor)*; Ellen Hopkins *(Clague Middle School, Ann Arbor)*; Teri Keusch *(Portland Middle School, Portland)*; Valerie Mills *(Oakland Schools, Waterford)*; Mary Beth Schmitt *(Traverse City East Junior High, Traverse City)*; Jack Smith *(Michigan State University, East Lansing)*; Rebecca Spencer *(Sparta Middle School, Sparta)*; Ann Marie Nicoll Turner *(Tappan Middle School, Ann Arbor)*; Scott Turner *(Scarlett Middle School, Ann Arbor)*

Minnesota

Margarita Alvarez *(Olson Middle School, Minneapolis)*; Jane Amundson *(Nicollet Junior High, Burnsville)*; Anne Bartel *(Minneapolis Public Schools)*; Gwen Ranzau Campbell *(Sunrise Park Middle School, White Bear Lake)*; Stephanie Cin *(Hidden Valley Elementary, Burnsville)*; Joan Garfield *(University of Minnesota, Minneapolis)*; Gretchen Hall *(Richfield Middle School, Richfield)*; Jennifer Larson *(Olson Middle School, Minneapolis)*; Michele Luke *(West Junior High, Minnetonka)*; Jeni Meyer *(Richfield Junior High, Richfield)*; Judy Pfingsten *(Inver Grove Heights Middle School, Inver Grove Heights)*; Sarah Shafer *(North Junior High, Minnetonka)*; Genni Steele *(Central Middle School, White Bear Lake)*; Victoria Wilson *(Eisenhower Elementary, Hopkins)*; Paul Zorn *(St. Olaf College, Northfield)*

New York

Debra Altenau-Bartolino *(Greenwich Village Middle School, New York)*; Doug Clements *(University of Buffalo)*; Francis Curcio *(New York University, New York)*; Christine Dorosh *(Clinton School for Writers, Brooklyn)*; Jennifer Rehn *(East Side Middle School, New York)*; Phyllis Tam *(IS 89 Lab School, New York)*; Marie Turini *(Louis Armstrong Middle School, New York)*; Lucy West *(Community School District 2, New York)*; Monica Witt *(Simon Baruch Intermediate School 104, New York)*

Pennsylvania

Robert Aglietti *(Pittsburgh)*; Sharon Mihalich *(Pittsburgh)*; Jennifer Plumb *(South Hills Middle School, Pittsburgh)*; Mary Lynn Raith *(Pittsburgh Public Schools)*

Texas

Michelle Bittick *(Austin Independent School District)*; Margaret Cregg *(Plano Independent School District)*; Sheila Cunningham *(Klein Independent School District)*; Judy Hill *(Austin Independent School District)*; Patricia Holguin *(El Paso Independent School District)*; Bonnie McNemar *(Arlington)*; Kay Neuse *(Plano Independent School District)*; Joyce Polanco *(Austin Independent School District)*; Marge Ramirez *(University of Texas at El Paso)*; Pat Rossman *(Baker Campus, Austin)*; Cindy Schimek *(Houston)*; Cynthia Schneider *(Charles A. Dana Center, University of Texas at Austin)*; Uri Treisman *(Charles A. Dana Center, University of Texas at Austin)*; Jacqueline Weilmuenster *(Grapevine-Colleyville Independent School District)*; LuAnn Weynand *(San Antonio)*; Carmen Whitman *(Austin Independent School District)*; James Wohlgehagen *(Plano Independent School District)*

Washington

Ramesh Gangolli *(University of Washington, Seattle)*

Wisconsin

Susan Lamon *(Marquette University, Hales Corner)*; Steve Reinhart *(retired, Chippewa Falls Middle School, Eau Claire)*

Table of Contents

Bits and Pieces I
Understanding Fractions, Decimals, and Percents

Bits and Pieces I

Understanding Fractions, Decimals, and Percents

Bryce and Rachel are collecting food for the local food bank. Bryce's goal is to collect 32 items. Rachel's goal is to collect 24 items. Suppose Rachel and Bryce each meet their goal. What fraction of Bryce's goal does Rachel collect?

Sarah and her uncle, Takota, go fishing in the Grand River. Each person catches one fish. Sarah's fish is $\frac{5}{8}$ of a foot long. Takota's fish is $\frac{2}{3}$ of a foot long. Which fish is longer?

A survey asked cat owners, "Does your cat have bad breath?" Out of the 200 cat owners surveyed, 80 answered yes to this question. What percent of the cat owners answered yes?

You often encounter situations in which a whole number cannot communicate information precisely. Sometimes you need to talk about parts of wholes: "What fraction of the students going on this trip are eighth-graders?" "Water occupies more than 71% of the Earth's surface." You also need a way to discuss how to share, divide, or measure things: "What part of the pizza will we each get?" or "How tall are you?" Fractions, decimals, and percents are all ways of expressing quantities or measures that are not whole numbers.

People have been working on ways to talk about fractions and to do operations with them for almost 4,000 years. A document written in Egypt around 1850 B.C. (now called the Moscow Papyrus) may contain the first record of people working with fractions. The word *fraction* comes from the Latin word *fractio*, which means "a breaking."

In *Bits and Pieces I*, you will develop skill with fractions, decimals, and percents. Your new skill can help you make sense of situations like the ones on the facing page.

Mathematical Highlights

Understanding Fractions, Decimals, and Percents

In *Bits and Pieces I*, you will explore relationships among fractions, decimals, and percents. You will learn that fractions and decimals are also part of a larger set of numbers called *rational numbers*.

You will learn how to

- Model situations involving fractions, decimals, and percents
- Understand and use equivalent fractions to reason about situations
- Compare and order fractions and decimals
- Move flexibly among fraction, decimal, and percent representations
- Use benchmarks, such as $0, \frac{1}{2}, 1, 1\frac{1}{2}$, and 2, to help estimate the size of a number or sum
- Develop and use benchmarks that relate different forms of rational numbers (for example, 50% is the same as $\frac{1}{2}$ or 0.5)
- Use context, physical models, drawings, patterns, or estimation to help reason about situations involving rational numbers

As you work on problems in this unit, ask yourself questions about situations that involve rational numbers and relationships:

What models or diagrams might be helpful in understanding the situation and the relationships among quantities?

Do I want to express the quantities in the situation as fractions, decimals, or percents?

What strategies can I use to find equivalent forms of fractions, decimals, or percents?

What strategies can I use to compare or order a set of fractions, decimals, and percents?

Investigation 1

Fundraising Fractions

Students at Thurgood Marshall Middle School are organizing three fundraising projects to raise money. The eighth-grade class will sell calendars, the seventh-grade class will sell popcorn, and the sixth-grade class will sell art, music, and sports posters. The three grades are competing to see which will reach its fundraising goal first.

1.1 Reporting Progress

The school's principal has a chart that looks like a thermometer in front of her office. The chart shows progress on the fundraising. She analyzes the progress shown on the thermometer using fractions and whole numbers. Then she announces the progress of the classes over the loudspeaker.

Problem 1.1 Whole Numbers and Fractions

A. Based on the thermometer at the right for Day 2, which of the following statements could the principal use to describe the sixth-graders' progress?

- The sixth-graders have raised $100.

- The sixth-graders have reached $\frac{1}{4}$ of their goal.

- The sixth-graders have reached $\frac{2}{8}$ of their goal.

- The sixth-graders only have $225 left to meet their goal.

- The sixth-graders have completed 50% of their goal.

- At this pace, the sixth-graders should reach their goal in six more days.

B. Make up two more statements the principal could use in the announcement.

C. 1. What are two claims the sixth-graders can make if they collect $15 on the third day?

2. Draw and shade the thermometer for Day 3.

ACE Homework starts on page 12.

Goal
$300

Day 2

Fractions like the ones the principal uses can be written using two whole numbers separated by a bar. For example, one half is written $\frac{1}{2}$ and two eighths is written $\frac{2}{8}$. The number above the bar is the **numerator,** and the number below the bar is the **denominator.**

As you work on the problems in this unit, think about what the numerators and denominators of your fractions are telling you about each situation.

1.2 Folding Fraction Strips

One way to think about fractions is to make fraction strips by folding strips of paper into fractional parts of equal size. In this problem you will fold fraction strips that can help you with other problems in the unit. As you are folding your strips, think about the strategies you use to make the different fraction strips.

Problem 1.2 Folding Fraction Strips

A. 1. Use strips of paper that are $8\frac{1}{2}$ inches long. Fold the strips to show halves, thirds, fourths, fifths, sixths, eighths, ninths, tenths, and twelfths. Mark the folds so you can see them better.

2. What strategies did you use to fold your strips?

B. 1. How could you use the halves strip to fold eighths?

2. How could you use the halves strip to fold twelfths?

C. What fraction strips can you make if you start with a thirds strip?

D. Which of the fraction strips you folded have at least one mark that lines up with the marks on the twelfths strip?

E. 1. Sketch a picture of a fifths strip and mark $\frac{1}{5}, \frac{2}{5}, \frac{3}{5}, \frac{4}{5}$, and $\frac{5}{5}$ on the strip.

2. Show $\frac{1}{10}, \frac{2}{10}, \frac{3}{10}, \frac{4}{10}, \frac{5}{10}, \frac{6}{10}, \frac{7}{10}, \frac{8}{10}, \frac{9}{10}$, and $\frac{10}{10}$ on the fifths strip that you sketched.

F. What do the numerator and denominator of a fraction tell you?

ACE Homework starts on page 12.

The thermometers on the next page show the progress of the sixth-grade poster sales after 2, 4, 6, 8, and 10 days. The principal needs to know what fraction of the goal the sixth-grade class has achieved after each day.

Problem 1.3 Finding Fractional Parts

A. Use the thermometers on the facing page. What fraction of their goal did the sixth-graders reach after each day?

B. What do the numerator and denominator of each fraction tell you about each thermometer?

C. What strategies did you use to estimate the fraction of the goal achieved for each day?

D. How much money had the sixth-graders raised at the end of each day?

E. At the end of Day 9, the sixth-graders had raised $240.

   1. What fraction of their goal had they reached?

   2. Show how you would shade a thermometer for Day 9 on a blank thermometer.

ACE Homework starts on page 12.

Sixth-Grade Fundraiser

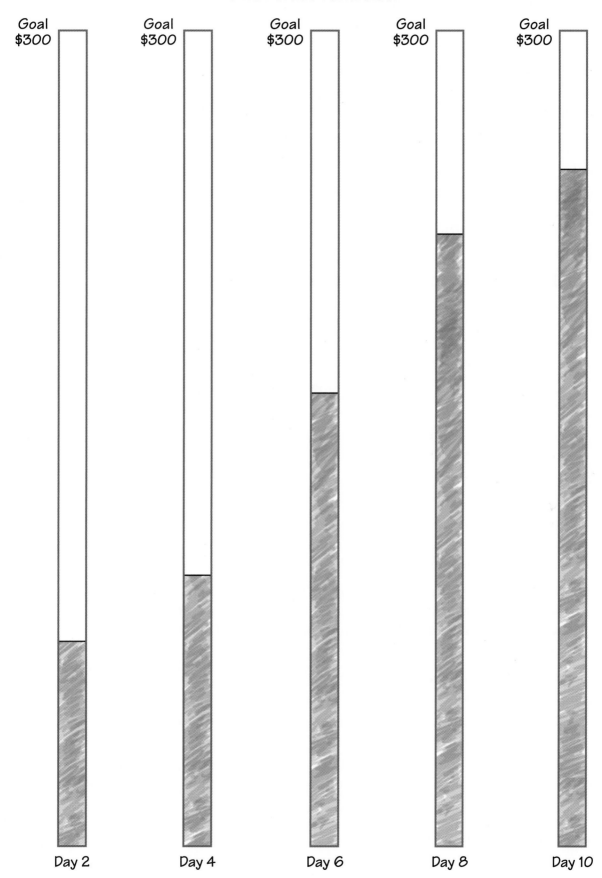

Goal $300   Goal $300   Goal $300   Goal $300   Goal $300

Day 2   Day 4   Day 6   Day 8   Day 10

1.4 Comparing Classes

At Thurgood Marshall Middle School, the seventh-grade class is larger than the sixth-grade class. The eighth-grade class is smaller than the sixth-grade class. Because they are different sizes, each class picked a different goal for its fundraiser.

The teachers decided to help the students with the fundraiser. The teachers sold books for summer reading and set a goal of $360. Each group made a thermometer to show its progress. The thermometers on the next page show the goals and the results for each group after ten days.

Problem 1.4 Using Fractions to Compare

A. 1. What fraction of their goal did each class and the teachers reach after Day 10 of the fundraiser?

   2. How much money did each group raise?

   3. Write number sentences to show how you found your answers in part (2).

B. 1. What could the president of each class say on the morning announcements to support a claim that his or her class did better than the other two?

   2. What do you think the teachers would say?

C. The shaded part of the sixth-grade thermometer is the same length as the shaded part of the teachers' thermometer. Does that mean they each reached the same fraction of their goal? Explain.

D. Gwen noticed that the one-half mark on the sixth-grade thermometer lines up with the eighth grade's progress on Day 10. Does this mean that the eighth-graders have achieved half of their goal on Day 10? Explain.

E. Make (or use) two blank thermometers the same length as the eighth-grade thermometer.

   1. Mark one thermometer with the sixth-grade goal. Then shade it to show the sixth-grade progress after Day 10.

   2. Mark the other thermometer with the seventh-grade goal. Then shade it to show the seventh-grade progress after Day 10.

   3. Describe your strategy for shading the thermometers.

ACE Homework starts on page 12.

Thurgood Marshall Middle School Fundraiser: Day 10

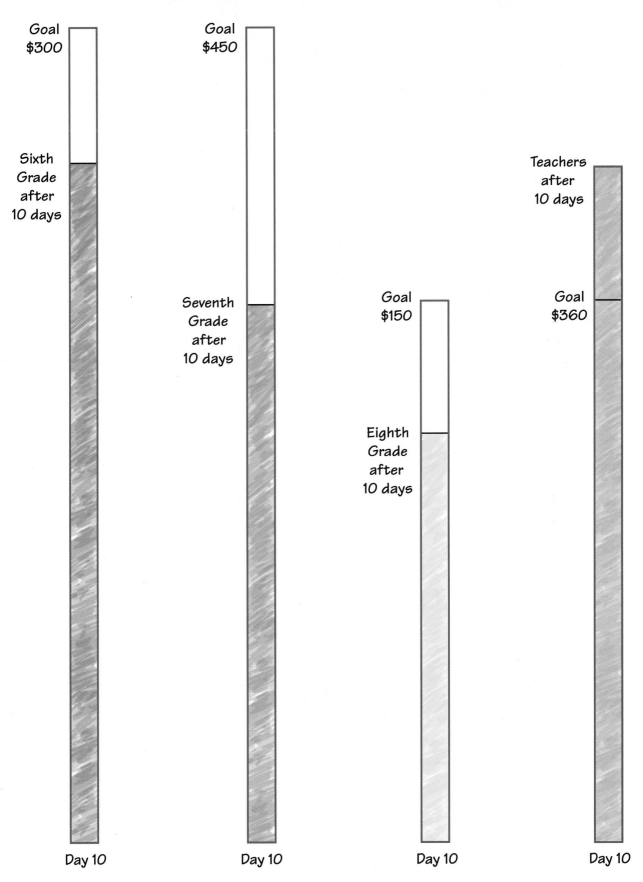

Goal
$300

Sixth
Grade
after
10 days

Day 10

Goal
$450

Seventh
Grade
after
10 days

Day 10

Goal
$150

Eighth
Grade
after
10 days

Day 10

Teachers
after
10 days

Goal
$360

Day 10

Applications

1. Mountview Middle School conducted the same type of fundraiser as Thurgood Marshall Middle School. The Mountview sixth-grade thermometer for Day 2 is shown at the right.

   a. Write three statements that the principal could make when reporting the results of the progress made by the sixth-graders.

   b. What are two claims that the sixth-graders could make if they collected $50 on the third day?

   c. Draw and shade a thermometer for Day 3.

2. a. What fraction strips could you make if you started with a fourths strip?

   b. If your teacher gave you an eighths strip like the one you made in Problem 1.2, which of the fraction strips you folded for Problem 1.2 would have more than one mark that lines up with the marks on the eighths strip?

Goal
$300

Day 2

For Exercises 3–6, fold fraction strips or use some other method to estimate the fraction of the fundraising thermometer that is shaded.

3.

Goal
$400

4.

Goal
$400

5.

Goal
$400

6.

Goal
$400

For Exercises 7–11, use this illustration of a drink dispenser. The gauge on the side of the dispenser shows how much of the liquid remains in the dispenser. The dispenser holds 120 cups.

7. **a.** About what fraction of the dispenser is filled with liquid?

   b. About how many cups of liquid are in the dispenser?

   c. About what fraction of the dispenser is empty?

   d. About how many more cups of liquid would it take to fill the dispenser?

8. For parts (a)–(c), sketch the gauge and tell whether each dispenser is *almost empty, about half full,* or *almost full.*

   a. five sixths $\left(\frac{5}{6}\right)$ of a full dispenser

   b. three twelfths $\left(\frac{3}{12}\right)$ of a full dispenser

   c. five eighths $\left(\frac{5}{8}\right)$ of a full dispenser

9. **Multiple Choice** Which gauge shows about 37 out of 120 cups remaining?

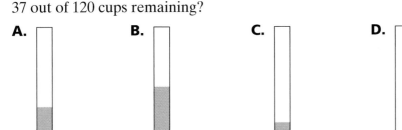

10. **Multiple Choice** Which gauge shows about 10 out of 120 cups remaining?

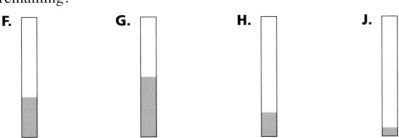

11. In Exercises 9 and 10, about what fraction is shaded in each gauge you chose?

12. Suppose you were trying to measure progress on a fundraising thermometer with your fifths strip, but the progress was between $\frac{3}{5}$ and $\frac{4}{5}$. What could you do to find a more exact answer?

For Exercises 13–15, use the information below.

You can also use fraction strips to name points on a number line. The point on this number line is at $\frac{1}{2}$.

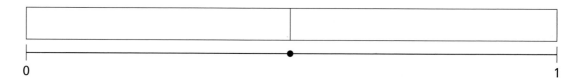

Copy each number line. Use fraction strips or some other method to name the point with a fraction.

13.

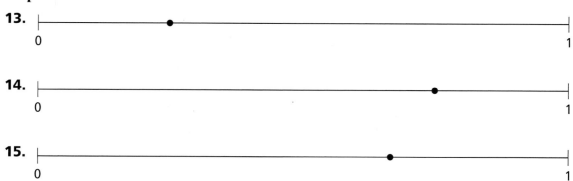

14.

15.

16. Samuel is getting a snack for himself and his little brother, Adam. Samuel takes half of one snack bar for himself and half of another snack bar for Adam. Adam complains that Samuel got more. Samuel says that he got half and Adam got half. What might be the problem?

17. In Problem 1.4, the eighth-grade thermometer is smaller than the sixth- and seventh-grade thermometers. Redraw the eighth-grade thermometer so that it is the same size as the sixth- and seventh-grade thermometers, but still shows the correct fraction for Day 10.

For: Help with Exercise 17
Web Code: ame-2117

18. If a class collects $155 toward a fundraising goal of $775, what fraction represents the class's progress toward its goal?

19. Bryce and Rachel are collecting food for the local food bank. Bryce's goal is to collect 32 items. Rachel's goal is to collect 24 items. If Rachel and Bryce each meet their goal, what fraction of Bryce's goal does Rachel collect?

Connections

20. Is 450 divisible by 5, 9, and 10? Explain.

21. Explain your answer to each question.
  a. Is 12 a divisor of 48?
  b. Is 4 a divisor of 150?
  c. Is 3 a divisor of 51?

22. Multiple Choice Choose the number that is not a factor of 300.
  A. 5   **B.** 6   **C.** 8   **D.** 20

23. Multiple Choice Choose the answer that shows all of the factors of 48.
  F. 2, 4, 8, 24, and 48   **G.** 1, 2, 3, 4, 5, and 6
  H. 48, 96, 144   **J.** 1, 2, 3, 4, 6, 8, 12, 16, 24, and 48

24. a. Miguel says that numbers that are divisible by 2 can easily be separated into halves of the number. Do you agree? Why or why not?
  b. Manny says that if Miguel is correct, then any numbers that are divisible by 3 can easily be separated into thirds. Do you agree? Why or why not?
  c. Lupe says that if any number is divisible by n, it can be easily separated into $n$ths. Do you agree with her? Explain.

25. a. If you had a fraction strip folded into twelfths, what fractional lengths could you measure with the strip?
  b. How is your answer in part (a) related to the factors of 12?

26. a. If you had a fraction strip folded into tenths, what fractional lengths could you measure with the strip?
  b. How is your answer in part (a) related to the factors of 10?

27. Ricky found a beetle that has a body one fourth $\left(\frac{1}{4}\right)$ the length of the fraction strips used in Problem 1.2.

   a. How many beetle bodies, placed end to end, would have a total length equal to the length of a fraction strip?

   b. How many beetle bodies, placed end to end, would have a total length equal to three fraction strips?

   c. Ricky drew 13 paper beetle bodies, end to end, each the same length as the one he found. How many fraction strips long is Ricky's line of beetle bodies?

For Exercises 28–30, use the bar graph below, which shows the number of cans of juice three sixth-grade classes drank.

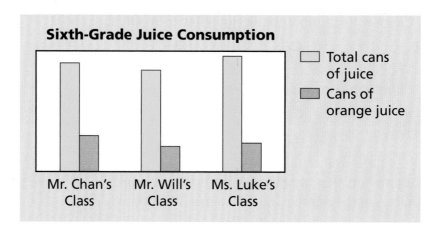

28. In each class, what fraction of the cans were orange juice?

29. In which class would you say orange juice was most popular?

30. a. Students in Mr. Chan's class drank a total of ten cans of orange juice. About how many cans of orange juice did the students in each of the other two classes drink?

   b. About how many total cans of juice did each of the three classes drink?

Extensions

31. Dario made three pizzas, which he sliced into quarters. After considering how many people he would be sharing with, he thought to himself, "Each person can have half."

    a. Is it possible that there was only one other person to share with? Explain.

    b. Is it possible that there were 5 other people to share with? Explain.

    c. Is it possible that there were 11 other people to share with?

For Exercises 32–35, copy the number line. Use fraction strips or some other method to name the point with a fraction.

32.

33.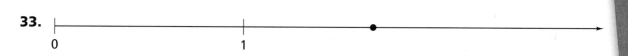

34.

35.

36. Write a numerator for each fraction to make the fraction close to, but not equal to, $\frac{1}{2}$. Then write a numerator to make each fraction close to, but greater than, 1.

    a. $\dfrac{\blacksquare}{22}$ b. $\dfrac{\blacksquare}{43}$ c. $\dfrac{\blacksquare}{17}$

37. Write a denominator to make each fraction close to, but not equal to, $\frac{1}{2}$. Then write a denominator to make each fraction close to, but greater than, 1.

    a. $\dfrac{22}{\blacksquare}$ b. $\dfrac{43}{\blacksquare}$ c. $\dfrac{17}{\blacksquare}$

Mathematical Reflections 1

In this investigation, you made fraction strips to help you identify fractional parts of a whole. These questions will help you summarize what you have learned.

Think about your answers to these questions. Discuss your ideas with other students and your teacher. Then write a summary of your findings in your notebook.

1. Two different classes reached $\frac{3}{5}$ of their fundraising goals. Did the two classes raise the same amount of money? Explain.

2. What do the numerator and the denominator of a fraction tell you?

3. If a class goes over its goal, what can you say about the fraction of their goal they have reached?

Investigation 2

Sharing and Comparing With Fractions

In Investigation 1, you used fraction strips to help determine what fraction of a fundraising goal students had reached. You interpreted fractions as parts of a whole. In this investigation, you will explore situations in which fractions are used to make comparisons.

2.1 Equivalent Fractions and Equal Shares

Sid and Susan are going hiking on the Appalachian Trail in Virginia with a group of friends. They are packing snack foods that are easy to carry and to eat. Their favorite is licorice (LIK uh rish) lace, a rope candy that looks like a long, round shoelace. Sid packs a licorice lace to share on the hike.

The licorice lace is 48 inches long and difficult to break into pieces. Sid can mark the licorice lace by cutting partway through. Then it will be easy to break and share later.

A. There are four people going on the hike. How should Sid mark the licorice lace so that each person can have a fair share? Draw a picture (making the drawing at least 4 inches long) and label one hiker's share of the lace.

B. Two more friends join the hike! Each wants a fair share of the licorice lace. Sid has to add more marks to the lace. He is stuck with the marks he has already made. Sid makes new marks so that the new marks together with the old marks make equal-size pieces.

    1. Draw a picture to show how Sid can add more marks to the licorice lace so it has equal-size pieces and can be broken to serve six people. Label one hiker's share.

    2. What fraction of the licorice lace will each of the six hikers get?

C. Well, you've probably guessed what happens next! Two more join the hike. Poor Sid has to re-mark the licorice lace he made for six people with additional marks. The new marks along with the old marks must form equal-size pieces to break off and share equally among eight friends. How should he re-mark the lace?

    1. Draw a picture and label one hiker's share of the licorice lace.

    2. How many inches of the lace will each of the eight hikers get?

How can I re-mark the licorice so all eight people get the same amount?

D. Use your drawing for Question C. Are there any marks that could be labeled with more than one fraction? If so, give some examples.

E. Carlotta bought a 48-inch blueberry lace. She cut off a part for her friend Brianna.

Blueberry Lace

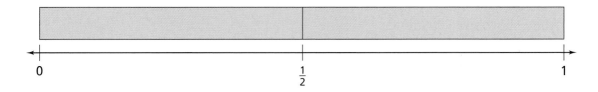

Brianna's part

1. What fraction of the blueberry lace did she give to Brianna?

2. How many inches of the blueberry lace did Brianna get?

ACE Homework starts on page 28.

2.2 Finding Equivalent Fractions

When you compare your fraction strips to each other, you find marks that match even though the total number of parts on each fraction strip is different. The places where marks match show **equivalent fractions.** Fractions that are equivalent represent the same amount even though their names are different.

Getting Ready for Problem 2.2

- Below is a fraction strip that shows a mark for $\frac{1}{2}$. What are five other fractions that are equivalent to $\frac{1}{2}$?

| 0 | $\frac{1}{2}$ | 1 |

A. 1. On a number line like the one below, carefully label marks that show where $\frac{1}{3}$ and $\frac{2}{3}$ are located.

$$0 \qquad\qquad\qquad \frac{1}{2} \qquad\qquad\qquad 1$$

2. Use the same number line. Mark the point that is halfway between 0 and $\frac{1}{3}$ and the point that is halfway between $\frac{2}{3}$ and 1.

3. Label these new marks with appropriate fraction names.

4. What are additional ways to label $\frac{1}{3}, \frac{1}{2}$, and $\frac{2}{3}$? Explain.

5. Use the same number line. Mark halfway between each of the marks that were already made.

6. Label the new marks on your number line. Add additional names to the marks that were already named.

7. Write three number sentences that show equivalent fractions on your number line. $\left(\text{Here is an example:} \frac{1}{2} = \frac{3}{6}.\right)$

8. Write two number sentences to show fractions that are equivalent to $\frac{9}{12}$.

B. 1. On your number line, the distance between the $\frac{1}{2}$ mark and the 1 mark is $\frac{1}{2}$ of a unit. The distance between the 0 mark and the $\frac{1}{3}$ mark on your number line is $\frac{1}{3}$ of a unit. Name two other fractions that are $\frac{1}{3}$ of a unit apart on your number line.

2. What is the distance between the $\frac{1}{3}$ and $\frac{1}{2}$ marks on your number line? How do you know?

3. Name at least two other fraction pairs that are the same distance apart as $\frac{1}{3}$ and $\frac{1}{2}$.

4. Describe the distance between $\frac{2}{3}$ and $\frac{5}{6}$ in two ways.

C. 1. Here is another number line with a mark for $\frac{7}{10}$ and for $\frac{3}{5}$. What is the distance between these two marks? On a copy of the number line, show how you know.

$$0 \qquad\qquad\qquad\qquad \frac{3}{5} \quad \frac{7}{10} \qquad 1$$

2. Suppose a number line is marked with tenths. Which marks can also be labeled with fifths?

D. 1. Find three fractions that are equivalent to $\frac{2}{7}$.

   2. Find every fraction with a whole-number denominator less than 50 that is equivalent to $\frac{10}{15}$.

   3. Describe a strategy for finding equivalent fractions.

   4. How does renaming fractions help you find distances between fractions?

ACE Homework starts on page 28.

Did You Know?

Hieroglyphic inscriptions show that, with the exception of $\frac{2}{3}$, Egyptian mathematicians only used fractions with 1 in the numerator. These fractions, such as $\frac{1}{2}$ and $\frac{1}{16}$, are known as *unit fractions*. Other fractions were expressed as sums of unit fractions. For example, the fraction $\frac{5}{12}$ was expressed as $\frac{1}{4} + \frac{1}{6}$ (as shown in the second and third pieces of the hieroglyphics below). Check with fraction strips to see if $\frac{1}{4} + \frac{1}{6} = \frac{5}{12}$.

Go Online
PHSchool.com
For: Information about hieroglyphics
Web Code: ame-9031

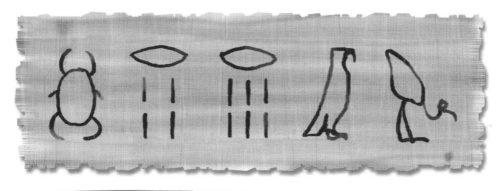

2.3 Comparing Fractions to Benchmarks

When you solve problems involving fractions, you may find it useful to estimate the size of fractions quickly. One way is to compare each fraction to $0, \frac{1}{2}$, and 1. These values serve as **benchmarks** —or reference points. First, you can decide whether a fraction is between 0 and $\frac{1}{2}$, between $\frac{1}{2}$ and 1, or greater than 1. Then decide whether the fraction is closest to $0, \frac{1}{2}$, or 1.

A. Decide whether each fraction below is in the interval between 0 and $\frac{1}{2}$, the interval between $\frac{1}{2}$ and 1, or between 1 and $1\frac{1}{2}$. Record your information in a table that shows which fractions are in each interval.

$$\frac{1}{5} \qquad \frac{4}{5} \qquad \frac{1}{3} \qquad \frac{2}{3} \qquad \frac{1}{10} \qquad \frac{6}{10} \qquad \frac{7}{10} \qquad \frac{8}{10} \qquad \frac{3}{8}$$

$$\frac{17}{12} \qquad \frac{7}{8} \qquad \frac{9}{8} \qquad \frac{7}{9} \qquad \frac{3}{4} \qquad \frac{3}{12} \qquad \frac{5}{6} \qquad \frac{3}{7} \qquad \frac{4}{7}$$

B. Decide whether each fraction above is closest to $0, \frac{1}{2}, 1,$ or $1\frac{1}{2}$. Record your information in a table that also includes the categories "Halfway Between 0 and $\frac{1}{2}$" and "Halfway Between $\frac{1}{2}$ and 1."

C. Compare each pair of fractions using benchmarks and other strategies. Then copy the fractions and insert the *less than* ($<$), *greater than* ($>$), or *equals* ($=$) symbol. Describe your strategies.

1. $\frac{5}{8} \ \blacksquare \ \frac{6}{8}$
2. $\frac{5}{6} \ \blacksquare \ \frac{5}{8}$
3. $\frac{2}{3} \ \blacksquare \ \frac{3}{9}$

4. $\frac{13}{12} \ \blacksquare \ \frac{6}{5}$
5. $\frac{6}{12} \ \blacksquare \ \frac{5}{9}$
6. $\frac{3}{4} \ \blacksquare \ \frac{12}{16}$

D. Use benchmarks and other strategies to help you write each set of fractions in order from least to greatest.

1. $\frac{2}{3}, \frac{7}{9}, \frac{3}{7}$
2. $\frac{4}{5}, \frac{4}{12}, \frac{7}{10}, \frac{5}{6}$

ACE Homework starts on page 28.

2.4 Fractions Between Fractions

Fractions seem to behave differently than whole numbers. For example, there is no whole number between 1 and 2. You already know that between $\frac{1}{4}$ and $\frac{1}{2}$ there are other fractions—for example, $\frac{1}{3}$.

As you do Problem 2.4, consider this question:
Can you always find another fraction between any two fractions?

Problem 2.4 Fractions Between Fractions

A. Find a fraction between each pair of fractions.

1. $\frac{3}{10}$ and $\frac{7}{10}$ **2.** $\frac{1}{5}$ and $\frac{2}{5}$

3. $\frac{1}{8}$ and $\frac{1}{4}$ **4.** $\frac{1}{10}$ and $\frac{1}{9}$

B. Find two fractions between each pair of fractions.

1. $\frac{4}{7}$ and $\frac{5}{7}$ **2.** $\frac{5}{11}$ and $\frac{6}{11}$

C. Describe the strategies you used in answering Questions A and B.

ACE   Homework starts on page 28.

2.5 Naming Fractions Greater Than 1

The whole numbers on a number line follow one another in a simple, regular pattern. Between every pair of whole numbers are many other points that may be labeled with fractions.

A number such as $2\frac{1}{2}$ is called a **mixed number** because it has a whole number part and a fraction part.

Getting Ready for Problem 2.5

- How would you label the marks halfway between the whole numbers on this number line?

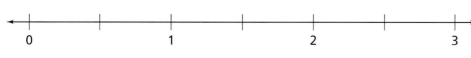

- Betty says that the mark between 2 and 3 should be labeled $\frac{1}{2}$. Do you agree? Why?

- If you made a new mark halfway between 2 and $2\frac{1}{2}$, how would you label it?

Alyssa asked whether a mixed number can be written as a fraction with no whole number part. For example,

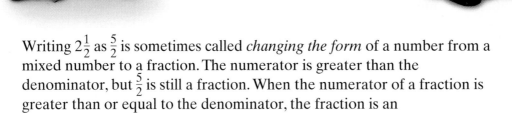

Alyssa: Can you write $2\frac{1}{2}$ as a fraction?

Sammy: Yeah, that's a good question.

Alyssa: Let's see. How many halves does the number 2 represent?

Sammy: Since there are two halves for each of the two wholes, 2 represents four halves.

Alyssa: Does knowing this help us write $2\frac{1}{2}$ as a fraction?

Sammy: Yes, now that we know that $2\frac{1}{2}$ represents five halves (4 + 1), we can write $2\frac{1}{2}$ as $\frac{5}{2}$.

Writing $2\frac{1}{2}$ as $\frac{5}{2}$ is sometimes called *changing the form* of a number from a mixed number to a fraction. The numerator is greater than the denominator, but $\frac{5}{2}$ is still a fraction. When the numerator of a fraction is greater than or equal to the denominator, the fraction is an **improper fraction.**

There is really nothing improper about such fractions! This is just a name used to distinguish between fractions less than 1 and those greater than 1.

Problem 2.5 Naming Fractions Greater Than 1

Each student activity group at Johnson School agreed to pick up litter along a 10-mile stretch of highway.

For each problem, use a number line to show what the problem describes and how you solved it. Show your answers as both a mixed number and an improper fraction.

A. Kate and Julianna are in the Marching Band. They work together to clean a section of highway that is $\frac{9}{4}$ miles long. Write this length as a mixed number.

B. The Math Club divided their 10-mile section into 2-mile segments that were assigned to the group members. Adrian and Ellie's section starts at the 2-mile point.

   1. If they start at the 2-mile point and clean for $\frac{5}{3}$ miles, how far are they from the start of the Math Club section? Explain.

   2. How many more miles of their 2-mile segment are left to clean?

C. The Drama Club's stretch of highway is very hilly and filled with litter. Working their hardest, club members can clean $1\frac{2}{3}$ miles each day.

   1. How far will they be at the end of the second day?

   2. At this rate, how many days will it take them to clean their 10-mile section?

   3. Jacqueline says that in four days they can clean $\frac{19}{3}$ miles. Thomas says they can clean $6\frac{2}{3}$ miles in four days. Who is right? Why?

D. The 10 miles assigned to the Chess Club start at the 10-mile point and go to the 20-mile point. When the Chess Club members have cleaned $\frac{5}{8}$ of their 10-mile section, between which miles will they be?

E. The Gardening Club has a section of highway between the 20- and 30-mile points. The club members set their goal for the first day to reach the 24-mile point. What fraction of the Gardening Club's total distance do they plan to cover on the first day?

ACE **Homework starts on page 28.**

Whole numbers, mixed numbers, and fractions all belong to the set of **rational numbers.** If you can write a number in fraction form using a whole number for each numerator and denominator $\left(\text{as in } \frac{3}{4}, \frac{5}{1}, \text{or } \frac{7}{2}\right)$, it is a rational number.

The word *rational* comes from the Latin word *ratio*, which means "relation." You will learn more about ratios and see other examples of rational numbers later in this unit.

Applications

1. Cheryl, Rita, and four of their friends go to a movie and share equally a 48-ounce bag of popcorn and three 48-inch licorice laces. Find the fraction of popcorn each gets and the fraction of licorice each gets.

2. The Lappans buy three large sandwich wraps to serve at a picnic. Nine people in all will be at the picnic. Show three different ways to cut the sandwiches so that each person gets an equal share.

3. Three neighbors are sharing a rectangular strip of land for a garden. They divide the land into 24 equal-sized pieces. What fraction of the land does each person get if they share it equally? Write the answer in more than one way.

For Exercises 4–7, decide whether the statement is *correct* or *incorrect*. Explain your reasoning in words or by drawing pictures.

4. $\frac{1}{3} = \frac{4}{12}$

5. $\frac{4}{6} = \frac{2}{3}$

6. $\frac{2}{5} = \frac{1}{3}$

7. $\frac{2}{5} = \frac{5}{10}$

For Exercises 8 and 9, draw fraction strips to show that the two fractions are equivalent.

8. $\frac{2}{5}$ and $\frac{6}{15}$

9. $\frac{1}{9}$ and $\frac{2}{18}$

Homework Help Online
PHSchool.com
For: Help with Exercise 8
Web Code: ame-2208

10. Write an explanation to a friend telling how to find a fraction that is equivalent to $\frac{3}{5}$. You can use words and pictures to help explain.

11. When you save or download a file, load a program, or open a page on the Internet, a status bar is displayed on the computer screen to let you watch the progress. Use the fraction strips shown to find three fractions that describe the status of the work in progress.

Downloading file ...

Compare each pair of fractions in Exercises 12–23 using benchmarks and other strategies. Then copy the fractions, and insert the *less than* (<), *greater than* (>), or *equals* (=) symbol.

12. $\frac{8}{10}$ ▨ $\frac{3}{8}$ **13.** $\frac{2}{3}$ ▨ $\frac{4}{9}$ **14.** $\frac{3}{5}$ ▨ $\frac{5}{12}$ **15.** $\frac{1}{3}$ ▨ $\frac{2}{3}$

16. $\frac{3}{4}$ ▨ $\frac{3}{5}$ **17.** $\frac{3}{2}$ ▨ $\frac{7}{6}$ **18.** $\frac{8}{12}$ ▨ $\frac{6}{9}$ **19.** $\frac{9}{10}$ ▨ $\frac{10}{11}$

20. $\frac{3}{12}$ ▨ $\frac{7}{12}$ **21.** $\frac{5}{6}$ ▨ $\frac{5}{8}$ **22.** $\frac{3}{7}$ ▨ $\frac{6}{14}$ **23.** $\frac{4}{5}$ ▨ $\frac{7}{8}$

Go Online
PHSchool.com

For: Multiple-Choice Skills
Practice
Web Code: ama-2254

24. Find a fraction between each pair of fractions.

   a. $\frac{1}{8}$ and $\frac{1}{4}$ **b.** $\frac{1}{6}$ and $\frac{1}{12}$ **c.** $\frac{1}{6}$ and $\frac{2}{6}$ **d.** $\frac{1}{4}$ and $\frac{2}{5}$

Between which two benchmarks $(0, \frac{1}{2}, 1, 1\frac{1}{2},$ and $2)$ does each fraction in Exercises 25–33 fall? Tell which is the nearer benchmark.

25. $\frac{3}{5}$ **26.** $1\frac{2}{6}$ **27.** $\frac{12}{10}$

28. $\frac{2}{18}$ **29.** $1\frac{8}{10}$ **30.** $1\frac{1}{10}$

31. $\frac{12}{24}$ **32.** $\frac{9}{6}$ **33.** $1\frac{12}{15}$

34. Describe, in writing or with pictures, how $\frac{7}{3}$ compares to $2\frac{1}{3}$.

35. Multiple Choice Which fraction is the greatest?

   A. $\frac{7}{6}$ **B.** $\frac{9}{8}$ **C.** $\frac{13}{12}$ **D.** $\frac{14}{15}$

36. Multiple Choice On a number line from 0 to 10, where is $\frac{13}{3}$ located?

    F. between 0 and 1   **G.** between 4 and 5

    H. between 5 and 6   **J.** between 6 and 7

37. Copy the number line below. Locate and label marks representing $\frac{9}{10}$, $\frac{11}{10}$, $2\frac{3}{10}$, and $2\frac{5}{10}$. For each point you mark, give two other fractions that are equivalent to the fraction given.

38. Copy the number line below. Locate and label marks representing $2\frac{1}{4}$, $1\frac{9}{10}$, and $\frac{15}{4}$.

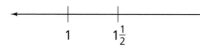

39. Copy the number line below. Locate and label a fraction represented by each point described.

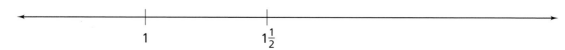

    a. a point close to but greater than 1

    b. a point close to but less than $1\frac{1}{2}$

    c. a point close to but greater than $1\frac{1}{2}$

    d. a point close to but less than 2

40. Copy the number line below. Locate and label marks representing 16, $15\frac{1}{2}$, $19\frac{1}{2}$, and $20\frac{1}{4}$.

41. Copy and complete the table.

Fraction	$\frac{5}{3}$	■	■	$\frac{19}{6}$	$\frac{37}{4}$	■
Mixed Number	■	$2\frac{4}{5}$	$9\frac{3}{7}$	■	■	$6\frac{2}{3}$

42. Kelly and Sean work together to clean a section of highway that is $\frac{10}{3}$ miles long. Write this distance as a mixed number.

43. The Chess Club is cleaning a very littered section of highway. Each day the members clean $1\frac{3}{4}$ miles of highway. After four days of hard work, Lakeisha says they have cleaned $\frac{28}{4}$ miles of highway. Glenda says they have cleaned 7 miles of roadway. Who is right? Why?

44. Change each mixed number into an improper fraction.

   a. $1\frac{2}{3}$ **b.** $6\frac{3}{4}$ **c.** $9\frac{7}{9}$ **d.** $4\frac{2}{7}$

45. Change each improper fraction into a mixed number.

   a. $\frac{22}{4}$ **b.** $\frac{10}{6}$ **c.** $\frac{17}{5}$ **d.** $\frac{36}{8}$

Connections

For Exercises 46 and 47, write a fraction to describe how much pencil is left, compared to a new pencil. Measure from the left edge of the eraser to the point of the pencil.

46.

47.

48. These bars represent trips that Ms. Axler took in her job this week.

300 km

180 km

200 km

a. Copy each bar and shade in the distance Ms. Axler traveled after going one third of the total distance for each trip.

b. How many kilometers had Ms. Axler traveled when she was at the one-third point in each trip? Explain your reasoning.

49. Multiple Choice Find the least common multiple of the following numbers: 3, 4, 5, 6, 10, and 15.

A. 1   **B.** 15   **C.** 60   **D.** 54,000

50. Use what you found in Exercise 49. Write the fractions in equivalent form, all with the same denominator.

$$\frac{1}{3} \qquad \frac{1}{4} \qquad \frac{1}{5} \qquad \frac{1}{6} \qquad \frac{1}{10} \qquad \frac{1}{15}$$

Find the greatest common factor of each pair of numbers.

51. 12 and 48   **52.** 6 and 9

53. 24 and 72   **54.** 18 and 45

Use your answers from Exercises 51–54 to write a fraction equivalent to each fraction given.

55. $\frac{12}{48}$ **56.** $\frac{6}{9}$ **57.** $\frac{24}{72}$ **58.** $\frac{18}{45}$

Extensions

For Exercises 59–64, copy each number line. Estimate and mark where the number 1 would be.

59.

0              $\frac{2}{5}$

60.

0                                 $\frac{9}{10}$

61.

```
  ┼──────────┼────────────────────────────────────→
  0          1/3
```

62.

```
  ┼──────────────────────────────────┼──────────────→
  0                                   5/2
```

63.

```
  ┼──────────────────────────────────┼──────────────→
  0                                   3/4
```

64.

```
  ┼──────────────────────────────┼──────────────────→
  0                              6/4
```

For Exercises 65–67, find every fraction with a denominator less than 50 that is equivalent to the given fraction.

65. $\dfrac{3}{15}$ **66.** $\dfrac{8}{3}$ **67.** $1\dfrac{4}{6}$

68. Use the information in *Did You Know?* after Problem 2.2 to figure out how to name the sums below with a single fraction. (Your strips might be helpful.) Explain your reasoning.

   a. $\dfrac{1}{2} + \dfrac{1}{4} = $ ■ **b.** $\dfrac{1}{12} + \dfrac{1}{6} = $ ■ **c.** $\dfrac{1}{4} + \dfrac{1}{6} + \dfrac{1}{12} = $ ■

69. A *unit fraction* is a fraction with 1 in the numerator. Find a set of unit fractions whose sum equals each of the following. Try to find more than one answer for each.

   a. $\dfrac{7}{8}$ **b.** $\dfrac{7}{12}$

70. Find five fractions between $\dfrac{8}{10}$ and $\dfrac{5}{4}$.

71. Does $\dfrac{4}{5}, \dfrac{17}{23}$, or $\dfrac{51}{68}$ represent the greatest part of a whole? Explain your reasoning.

72. Copy the number line below. Locate and label marks representing $0, \dfrac{3}{4}$, $\dfrac{1}{8}$, and $2\dfrac{2}{3}$.

```
  ←────────────────────┼──────┼──────────────────────→
                       1     1¼
```

Mathematical Reflections 2

In this investigation, you explored equivalent fractions, compared fractions to benchmarks, and considered fractions greater than 1. These questions will help you summarize what you have learned.

Think about your answers to these questions. Discuss your ideas with other students and your teacher. Then write a summary of your findings in your notebook.

1. Describe your strategy for finding a fraction equivalent to a given fraction.

2. Describe strategies you have found for deciding whether a fraction is between 0 and $\frac{1}{2}$ or between $\frac{1}{2}$ and 1.

3. Explain how you can decide which of two fractions is greater.

4. Describe how to write a mixed number as a fraction.

5. Describe how to write a fraction greater than 1 as a mixed number.

Moving Between Fractions and Decimals

You see decimals every day, in lots of different places. Can you tell where each of the decimals below was found?

3.1 Making Smaller Parts

Decimals give us a way to write special fractions that have denominators of 10 or 100 or 1,000 or 10,000 or even 100,000,000,000. In Investigation 1, you folded fraction strips. One of the strips you made was a tenths strip, shown on the next page.

Suppose you need more marks to show a fraction. Look at the tenths strip.

- How could you fold a tenths strip to get a hundredths strip?
- How would you label this new fraction strip?

A *tenths grid* is also divided into ten equal parts. It resembles a tenths fraction strip, but it is square. Below is a tenths grid that shows the fraction and its decimal equivalent represented by each section of the grid.

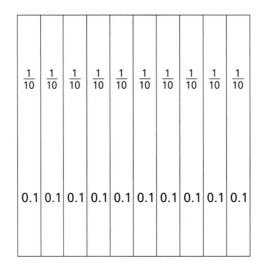

Here are some examples of fractions represented on tenths grids. The fraction name and decimal name for the shaded part are given below each drawing.

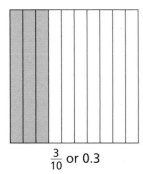

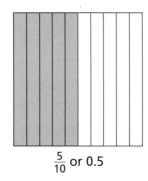

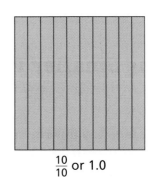

$\frac{3}{10}$ or 0.3 $\frac{5}{10}$ or 0.5 $\frac{10}{10}$ or 1.0

You can further divide a tenths grid by drawing horizontal lines to make ten rows. This makes 100 parts. This is called a *hundredths grid*.

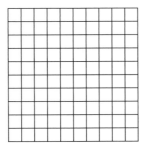

Fractions can also be represented on a hundredths grid. You can write fractional parts of 100 as decimal numbers, as in the following examples:

Fraction	Decimal	Representation on a Hundredths Grid
$\frac{7}{100}$	0.07	
$\frac{27}{100}$	0.27	
$\frac{20}{100}$	0.20	

A. 1. Mark and label the fractions $\frac{1}{4}$, $\frac{2}{4}$, $\frac{3}{4}$, and $\frac{4}{4}$ on a hundredths fraction strip like the one shown.

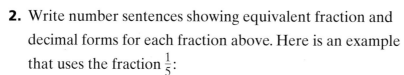

2. After marking each fraction, shade that fraction on a hundredths grid like the one at the right.

3. Write a fraction that shows how many hundredths you shaded.

4. Write a decimal that shows how many hundredths you shaded.

B. 1. Which of the fractions could be easily shown on a tenths grid or a tenths fraction strip?

2. Write number sentences showing equivalent fraction and decimal forms for each fraction above. Here is an example that uses the fraction $\frac{1}{5}$:

$$\frac{1}{5} = \frac{2}{10} = 0.2 \text{ and } \frac{1}{5} = \frac{20}{100} = 0.20$$

C. Rewrite the fractions below using denominators of 10 or 100. Then, write a decimal for each fraction.

1. $\frac{2}{5}$ **2.** $\frac{26}{50}$ **3.** $\frac{4}{20}$ **4.** $\frac{4}{5}$

D. Lin, a sixth-grader at Pleasant Valley School, won a giant fruit bar for selling the most posters in the school fundraiser. The bar is 10 inches by 10 inches and is marked into 100 square-inch sections. Lin decides to share her fruit bar with some friends.

1. Lin gives 0.1 of the bar to Bailey. Describe two ways Lin could cut the bar to share it with Bailey.

2. Lin gives 0.25 of the bar to Lula. Describe two ways that she could cut the bar to share it with Lula.

3. Lin gives $\frac{1}{5}$ of the bar to her little sister, Donna, who helped her sell the posters for the fundraiser. Write two decimals that represent how much of the bar Donna gets.

4. Lin gives $\frac{1}{50}$ of the bar to Patrick. Write a decimal that represents how much of the bar Patrick gets.

5. Shade a hundredths grid to show one way that Lin could cut all of the sections to give to her friends.

6. Who got more of the fruit bar—Bailey, Lula, Donna, or Patrick? Explain.

7. How much of the bar was left for Lin?

ACE **Homework starts on page 47.**

3.2 Making Even Smaller Parts

The place value chart below shows a set of special numbers in both fraction and decimal form. Think about these questions as you look at the chart:

What do you notice about the denominators of the fractions as you move to the right from the decimal point?

Why are these denominators useful in writing fractions as decimals?

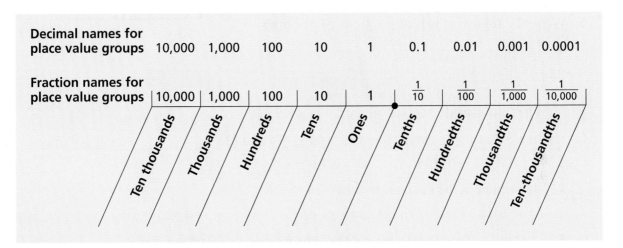

Some fractions can be written as decimals using only the tenths place.

$$\frac{4}{5} = \frac{8}{10} = 0.8$$

Some fractions, like $\frac{1}{4}$, are difficult to represent with tenths. You can write $\frac{1}{4}$ as an equivalent fraction with a denominator of 100 to find the decimal representation.

$$\frac{1}{4} = \frac{25}{100} = 0.25$$

You can think of $\frac{1}{4}$ as 25 hundredths or as 2 tenths and 5 hundredths. For some fractions, you may need to section a grid into even more parts to represent denominators such as 1,000 or 10,000.

- What might a hundredths grid look like if each square were subdivided into 10 equal parts? How many parts would the new grid have?

- What is a fraction name for the smallest part of this new grid? What is its decimal name?

Problem 3.2 Place Values Greater Than Hundredths

A. 1. What fraction of the grid at the right is shaded?

2. How many hundredths are shaded? Write your answer as a fraction and as a decimal.

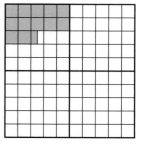

3. If you shaded the same fraction on a *thousandths grid,* how many thousandths would be shaded? Write your answer as a fraction and as a decimal.

B. Write the following sets of fractions as decimals.

1. $\frac{9}{10}$, $\frac{9}{100}$, $\frac{9}{1,000}$, $\frac{9}{10,000}$

2. $\frac{43}{10}$, $\frac{43}{100}$, $\frac{43}{1,000}$, $\frac{43}{10,000}$

3. What patterns do you see in parts (1) and (2)?

C. Use the following decimals to answer parts (1) and (2).

0.23	0.7011	2.7011	0.00006

1. Write each of the decimal numbers in words.

2. Write each of the decimal numbers as fractions or mixed numbers.

D. For each pair of numbers, find another number that is between them.

1. 0.8 and 0.85   **2.** 0.72 and 0.73

3. 1.2 and 1.205   **4.** 0.0213 and 0.0214

5. Describe one strategy that you used to find numbers between decimals in parts (1)–(4).

ACE Homework starts on page 47.

3.3 Decimal Benchmarks

Below are representations of $\frac{3}{4}$ on a hundredths grid and on a number line.

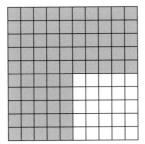

0   1

Consider these questions:

Each representation shows that $\frac{3}{4}$ is 75 out of 100 parts. How would you write this as a decimal?

Different representations are usually good for different things. Which representation, the grid or the number line, do you find most useful?

Sometimes knowing a little can go a long way! With decimals and fractions, knowing just a few fractions and their decimal equivalents can help you think about many other fractions and their decimal equivalents. In Problem 3.3 you will make a list of benchmarks that show equivalent fractions and decimals.

Mary wants to make a list of decimal benchmarks for these fraction benchmarks:

$$\frac{1}{2} \qquad \frac{1}{3} \qquad \frac{1}{4} \qquad \frac{1}{5} \qquad \frac{1}{6} \qquad \frac{1}{8} \qquad \frac{1}{10}$$

A. 1. For which of Mary's benchmark fractions do you already know the decimal equivalent? Show how you know.

2. Use hundredths grids to find decimals that represent or are close approximations for the ones you do not know.

3. Compare your decimals for $\frac{1}{4}$ and $\frac{1}{8}$.

4. Compare your decimals for $\frac{1}{3}$ and $\frac{1}{6}$.

B. Use your work with Mary's benchmark list to help you find decimal equivalents for the following groups of fractions:

1. $\frac{2}{5}$ $\qquad \frac{3}{5}$ $\qquad \frac{4}{5}$ $\qquad \frac{6}{5}$

2. $\frac{2}{8}$ $\qquad \frac{3}{8}$ $\qquad \frac{4}{8}$ $\qquad \frac{5}{8}$ $\qquad \frac{6}{8}$ $\qquad \frac{7}{8}$

3. $\frac{4}{20}$ $\qquad \frac{2}{6}$ $\qquad \frac{3}{12}$ $\qquad \frac{3}{6}$

4. Describe strategies you used to find decimal equivalents.

C. Which fraction benchmark is each decimal nearest?

1. 0.18   **2.** 0.46   **3.** 0.225   **4.** 0.099

5. Describe one strategy that you used to find answers to parts (1)–(4).

ACE Homework starts on page 47.

Did You Know?

Fractions like $\frac{1}{2}, \frac{1}{4}, \frac{1}{5}$, and $\frac{1}{10}$ all can be represented easily by decimals. However, a fraction such as $\frac{1}{3}$ requires careful thinking. It is easy to see that $\frac{1}{3}$ is between 0.3 and 0.4, and also between 0.33 and 0.34. We could go on and see that $\frac{1}{3}$ is between 0.333 and 0.334.

Where do we stop and get an exact value? It turns out that we do not *ever* get an exact answer if we stop finding additional decimal places! To write something like an exact value, we would need to write $\frac{1}{3}$ as 0.33333 . . . , where the ". . ." means that we go on and on, without stopping. When we need to stop somewhere, we write approximations for fractions. We often approximate $\frac{1}{3}$ by decimals such as 0.33, 0.333, or even 0.3333. We can use as many 3's as we need for whatever accuracy is appropriate.

3.4 Moving From Fractions to Decimals

In August 2004, Hurricane Charley swept though Cuba, Jamaica, and Florida. It destroyed many homes and caused lots of damage to land and buildings. Many people had no place to live and little clothing and food. In response, people from all over collected clothing, household items, and food to send to the victims of the hurricane.

One group of students decided to collect food to distribute to families whose homes were destroyed. They packed what they collected into boxes to send to the families. The students had to solve some problems while they were packing the boxes.

The students had 14 boxes for packing the food they collected. They wanted to share the supplies equally among the 14 families who would receive the boxes. They had bags and plastic containers to repack items for the individual boxes. They also had a digital scale that measured in kilograms or grams. (Remember that 1 kilogram = 1,000 grams.)

Food We Collected

42 kilograms of wheat crackers

77 kilograms of powdered milk

91 kilograms of peanut butter

21 kilograms of cheddar cheese

10.5 kilograms of Swiss Cheese

475 apples

195 oranges

7 kilograms of raisins

13 kilograms of saltine crackers

39 kilograms of animal crackers

A. How much of each item should the students include in each box? Explain how you found your answer.

B. One student calculated the amount of powdered milk by writing $\frac{77}{14}$, then $\frac{11}{2}$, or 5.5 kilograms per box. Use this method to calculate the amount of the other items per box.

C. Another student calculated the amount of Swiss cheese to include in each box by entering 10.5 into her calculator and dividing by 14. Is this a good method? Why or why not?

D. How does this problem suggest a way to change a fraction to a decimal? Explain.

ACE **Homework starts on page 47.**

3.5 Ordering Decimals

The decimal number system is based on place value. The value of a digit in a number depends on the place where it is written. So the "2" in "20" has a different meaning from the "2" in "0.02." The chart below shows the place value for each digit of the number 5,620.301.

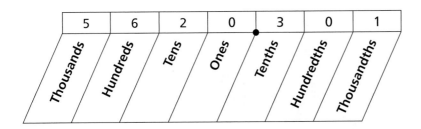

When you read decimal numbers that are greater than one, you say "and" to separate the whole number and decimal parts. For 2.5 you say "2 *and* 5 tenths."

Getting Ready for Problem

Consider these numbers:

> 2   0.2   20   0.00002

- How does place value tell you which number is greatest?

Decimals can also help you to answer questions like the following:

How tall am I?

Who is the tallest person in our class?

How many people are injured by doors every year?

As you work with decimals in this problem, think about place value and how it helps you to sort numbers.

Problem 3.5 Ordering Decimals

A. The table at the right shows the heights of a class of sixth-graders.

   1. Write Beth and Lana's heights as fractions. Who is taller?

   2. Order the students according to height from the shortest to the tallest.

Students' Heights

Student	Height (m)
Alan	1.45
Beth	1.52
Juan	1.72
Dave	1.24
Eddie	1.22
Fred	1.66
Greg	1.3
Hiroko	1.26
Abey	1.63
Joan	1.58
Karl	1.23
Lana	1.5
Maria	1.27

B. The federal government keeps track of all kinds of interesting data. The table at the right shows the number of people injured by various household items in a recent year per thousand U.S. residents.

   1. Order these items by the number of people injured from the least to the greatest.

   2. Which are more dangerous: beds or carpets? How do you know?

   3. Which item injured about twice as many people as ladders?

   4. Which item injured about 10 times as many people as televisions?

C. What strategies did you use to order and compare the decimals in each situation?

ACE Homework starts on page 47.

Injuries From Household Items

Item	People Injured (per thousand U.S. residents)
Bathtubs and showers	0.674
Beds	1.569
Carpets and rugs	0.404
Ceilings and walls	0.894
Chairs	1.008
Doors	1.143
Ladders	0.563
Tables	1.051
Televisions	0.140
Toilets	0.195
Windows	0.446

SOURCE: U.S. Census Bureau. Go to **www.PHSchool.com** for a data update. Web Code: amg-9041

Applications

For Exercises 1–5, the whole is one hundredths grid. Write fraction and decimal names for the shaded part.

1.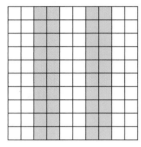

2.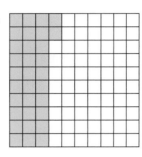

3.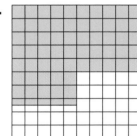

4.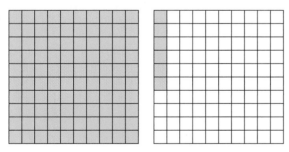

5.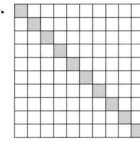

6. Name three fractions whose decimal equivalent is 0.25. Explain how you know each fraction is equivalent to 0.25. Draw a picture if it helps you explain your thinking.

7. Name three fractions whose decimal equivalent is 0.40. Explain how you know each fraction is equivalent to 0.40. Draw a picture if it helps you explain.

8. In parts (a)–(f), use blank hundredths grids to shade the given fractional part. Write the fraction as an equivalent decimal.

   a. $\frac{1}{2}$ of the hundredths grid

   b. $\frac{3}{4}$ of the hundredths grid

   c. $\frac{99}{100}$ of the hundredths grid

   d. $1\frac{3}{10}$ of the hundredths grids

   e. $2\frac{7}{10}$ of the hundredths grids

   f. $1\frac{3}{5}$ of the hundredths grids

Write a fraction equivalent to each decimal.

9. 0.08   10. 0.4   11. 0.04   12. 0.84

Go Online
PHSchool.com

For: Multiple-Choice Skills Practice
Web Code: ama-2354

Write a decimal equivalent for each fraction.

13. $\frac{3}{4}$ 14. $\frac{7}{50}$ 15. $\frac{13}{25}$ 16. $\frac{17}{25}$ 17. $\frac{1}{20}$ 18. $\frac{7}{10}$

For Exercises 19–21, copy the part of the number line given. Then find the "step" by determining the difference from one mark to another. Label the unlabeled marks with decimal numbers.

Sample

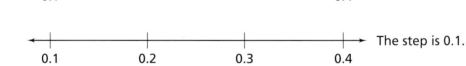

The step is 0.1.

0.1   0.2   0.3   0.4

19.
0.15   0.17

20.
0.028   0.029

21.
1.8   2.1

22. For each pair of numbers, find another number that is between them.

   a. 0.7 and 0.75

   b. 0.65 and 0.68

   c. 1.4 and 1.410

   d. 0.0322 and 0.323

23. Write each decimal in words.

    a. 3.620   **b.** 0.14   **c.** 0.00002

24. Name each decimal as a fraction or mixed number.

    a. 3.4   **b.** 0.35   **c.** 7.0003

25. For parts (a)–(c), use number lines to show the given fractional amount. Write the fraction as an equivalent decimal.

    a. $\frac{20}{25}$ **b.** $\frac{5}{8}$ **c.** $\frac{13}{26}$

26. Pilar divided 1 by 9 on her calculator and found that $\frac{1}{9}$ was approximately 0.1111. Find decimal approximations for each of the following fractions.

    a. $\frac{2}{9}$ **b.** $\frac{11}{9}$ **c.** $\frac{6}{9}$ **d.** $\frac{2}{3}$

    e. Describe any patterns that you see.

27. Ella says that she can find the decimal equivalent for lots of fractions because she knows that the decimal equivalent for $\frac{1}{5}$ is 0.2. Name three fractions for which Ella could find the decimal equivalent. Explain how Ella would use $\frac{1}{5}$ to find the decimal for each fraction.

28. Which fraction benchmark below is each decimal nearest?

    $\frac{1}{2}$ $\frac{1}{3}$ $\frac{1}{4}$ $\frac{1}{5}$ $\frac{1}{6}$ $\frac{1}{8}$ $\frac{1}{10}$

    a. 0.30   **b.** 0.50   **c.** 0.12333   **d.** 0.15

29. a. Sarah and her uncle, Takota, went fishing in the Grand River, and each caught one fish. Sarah's fish was $\frac{5}{8}$ of a foot long and Takota's was $\frac{2}{3}$ of a foot long. Which fish is longer? Explain.

    b. If Sarah and Takota measured their fish in decimals, would it be easier for them to tell which fish is longer? Explain.

30. Belinda used her calculator to find the decimal for the fraction $\frac{21}{28}$. When she entered $21 \div 28$, the calculator gave an answer that looked familiar. Why do you think she recognized it?

31. Multiple Choice The orchestra at Johnson School is responsible for cleaning a 15-mile section of highway. There are 45 students in the orchestra. If each orchestra member cleans an equal section, what decimal represents this section?

A. 0.3   **B.** 0.33   **C.** 0.3333 . . .   **D.** 3.0

32. Suppose a new student starts school today and your teacher asks you to teach her how to find decimal equivalents for fractions. What would you tell her? How would you convince her that your method works?

Copy each pair of numbers in Exercises 33–42. Insert <, >, or = to make a true statement.

33. 0.205 ▨ 0.21   **34.** 0.1 ▨ 0.1000

35. 0.04 ▨ 0.050   **36.** 1.03 ▨ 0.03

37. $\frac{5}{10}$ ▨ 0.6   **38.** $\frac{3}{5}$ ▨ 0.3

39. 0.4 ▨ $\frac{2}{5}$ **40.** 0.7 ▨ $\frac{1}{2}$

41. 0.52 ▨ $\frac{2}{4}$ **42.** 0.41 ▨ 0.405

43. For each pair of numbers in Exercises 33–42, write a number that is between the two given numbers. If this is not possible, explain why.

44. Which is greater, 0.45 or 0.9? Explain your reasoning. Draw a picture if it helps explain your thinking.

45. Which is greater, seventy-five hundredths or six tenths? Explain. Draw a picture if needed.

46. Which is greater, 0.6 or 0.60? Explain. Draw a picture if needed.

For Exercises 47–50, rewrite the numbers in order from least to greatest.

47. 0.33, 0.12, 0.127, 0.2, $\frac{45}{10}$ **48.** $\frac{45}{10}$, $\frac{3}{1,000}$, 0.005, 0.34

49. 0.418, $\frac{4}{10}$, $\frac{40}{1,000}$, 0.481   **50.** 0.827, 1.23, $\frac{987}{100}$, $\frac{987}{1,000}$

Homework Help Online
PHSchool.com

For: Help with Exercise 47
Web Code: ame-2347

Connections

51. Ten students went to a pizza parlor together. They ordered eight small pizzas.

    a. How much will each student receive if they share the pizzas equally? Express your answer as a fraction and as a decimal.

    b. Explain how you thought about the problem. Draw a picture that would convince someone that your answer is correct.

52. If you look through a microscope that makes objects appear ten times larger, 1 centimeter on a metric ruler looks like this:

0   1

    a. Copy this microscope's view of 1 cm. Divide the length for 1 cm into ten equal parts. What fraction of the "centimeter" does each of these parts represent?

    b. Now think of dividing one of these smaller parts into ten equal parts. What part of the original "centimeter" does each of the new segments represent?

    c. If you were to divide one of these new small parts into ten parts again, what part of the original "centimeter" would each of the new small parts represent?

53. Copy the number line below. Show 0.4 and 0.5 on your number line.

0   1

    a. Can you place five numbers between 0.4 and 0.5? If yes, place them on your number line with labels. If no, explain why not.

    b. Now, enlarge the line segment from 0.4 to 0.5. Make your new line segment approximately the length of the original number line. Place 0.4, 0.45, and 0.50 on your new number line. Can you find five numbers that belong between 0.45 and 0.50? If yes, place them on your number line with labels. If no, explain why not.

54. Hana says division should be called a "sharing operation." Why might she say this?

Extensions

For Exercises 55–60, find an estimate if you cannot find an exact answer. You may find that drawing a number line, a hundredths grid, or some other diagram is useful in solving the problem. Explain your reasoning.

55. What is $\frac{1}{4}$ of 12?　　　　**56.** What is $\frac{3}{4}$ of 8?

57. What is $\frac{2}{9}$ of 18?　　　　**58.** What is $\frac{2}{9}$ of 3?

59. What is $\frac{1}{4}$ of 3?　　　　**60.** What is $\frac{3}{4}$ of 3?

Mathematical Reflections 3

In this investigation, you studied relationships between fractions and decimals. These questions will help you summarize what you have learned.

Think about your answers to these questions. Discuss your ideas with other students and your teacher. Then write a summary of your findings in your notebook.

1. Describe how to find a decimal equivalent to a given fraction. How can you check your strategy to see that it works?

2. Describe how to find a fraction equivalent to a given decimal. Explain why your strategy works.

3. When comparing two decimals—such as 0.57 and 0.559—how can you decide which decimal represents the greater number?

Working With Percents

In this unit you have represented quantities as fractions and decimals to make sense of questions asking "how much?" or "how good?" or "which is better?" Below is a typical situation where a comparison is needed.

Getting Ready for Problem

When voters pass a school bond, they agree to a tax increase to pay for school construction. Based on the following data from a survey, which neighborhood—Whitehills or Bailey—is more positive about the proposed school bond to build a new gymnasium?

People Favorable to School Bond

Neighborhood	Yes	No
Whitehills	31	69
Bailey	17	33

To make meaningful comparisons in a situation like this, you need to rewrite the amounts so that you are using a common unit of comparison. One way to compare this data would be to figure out what the numbers in each neighborhood would be if 100 people were polled and the rate of support stayed the same. Think about how this might be done.

Fractions that have 100 as their denominator are very useful because you can easily write such fractions as decimals and then compare them to other decimals.

Another useful way to express a fraction with a denominator of 100 is to use a special symbol called the percent symbol—%. **Percent** means "out of 100." So, 8% means 8 out of 100.

In the fifteenth century, the phrase *per cento* stood for "per 100." Writing "per cento" over and over again probably got tiresome. Manuscripts on arithmetic from about 1650 show that people began to replace "per cento" with "per $\frac{0}{0}$" or "p $\frac{0}{0}$."

Later, the "per" was dropped and the symbol $\frac{0}{0}$ appeared alone.

Over time, $\frac{0}{0}$ became the symbol % which we use today.

Go Online
PHSchool.com **For:** Information about early arithmetic manuscripts
Web Code: ame-9031

4.1 Who's the Best?

Sports statistics are often given in percents. An important statistic for basketball players is their successful free-throw percent. Two well-known players are Yao Ming and Shaquille O'Neal. Mathematics can help us to compare their basketball statistics.

During a recent year, Yao Ming made 301 out of 371 free-throw attempts and Shaquille O'Neal made 451 out of 725 attempts. It is hard from these raw numbers to tell who was better at free throws. But in sports, the announcers give these raw numbers as percents.

A. Will said that he drew some pictures to help him think about the percent of free throws made by Yao Ming and Shaquille O'Neal, but then he got stuck! Here are Will's pictures.

1. Describe one way that Will could use his pictures to estimate the percentage of free throws made by each player.

2. Where would the mark for 50% be on the bottom scale in each picture?

3. Estimate the number that should sit on the top scale above 50% in each picture.

4. For each player, estimate the position for the mark representing the number of free throws made. Use a benchmark fraction to describe this location.

B. Alisha says that it is easy to tell who has the best free-throw record. She says, "Yao Ming made 301 free throws and Shaquille O'Neal made 451. So, Shaquille O'Neal has the better record!" Do you agree? Why or why not?

ACE Homework starts on page 61.

4.2 Choosing the Best

The Portland Tigers are playing the Coldwater Colts in basketball. The game is tied 58 to 58, but in the excitement both coaches step onto the court just as the buzzer sounds. A referee calls a technical foul on each coach.

Each coach has to choose one player to make the free-throw attempt. The winning team may be determined by the free throw.

Problem  Using Percents to Compare

A. The Portland coach will choose among three players to make the free-throw attempt. In their pre-game warm-ups:

- Angela made 12 out of 15 free throws

- Emily made 15 out of 20 free throws

- Cristina made 13 out of 16 free throws

Which player should the Portland coach select to make the free-throw attempt? Explain your reasoning.

B. The coach of the Coldwater Colts must choose the best player for free throws from the four players listed below. Which player should the coach select? Explain.

- Naomi made 10 out of 13 free throws

- Bobbie made 8 out of 10 free throws

- Kate made 36 out of 50 free throws

- Carmen made 16 out of 20 free throws

C. Find a way to support your conclusions in A and B that uses percents. What is the advantage of using percents when making comparisons?

ACE Homework starts on page 61.

Basketball was invented in 1891 by James Naismith. He was a physical education teacher who wanted to create a team sport that could be played indoors during the winter. The game was originally played with a soccer ball, peach baskets, and a ladder.

For: Information about the origins of basketball
Web Code: ame-9031

4.3 Finding a General Strategy

One of the powerful things about mathematics is that you can often find ways to solve one problem that can also be used to solve similar problems.

For example, it is easy to find percents when exactly 100 people are surveyed, since percent means "out of 100." However, surveys often involve more than or fewer than 100 people. Here is an example.

A survey asked cat owners, "Does your cat have bad breath?" Out of the 200 cat owners surveyed, 80 answered yes to this question. What percent of the cat owners answered yes?

Problem 4.3 Expressing Data in Percent Form

As you work on these questions, try to find a way to describe strategies you can use for solving these kinds of problems.

A. Suppose 80 out of 400 cat owners surveyed said their cats have bad breath. What percent of the cat owners is this? Is this percent greater than, equal to, or less than the percent represented by 80 out of 200 cat owners? Explain.

B. If 120 out of 300 seventh-graders surveyed said mathematics is their favorite subject, how would you express this as a fraction? Write this fraction as a decimal and as a percent.

C. Suppose 30 out of 50 adults surveyed said they enjoy their jobs. How would you express this as a fraction, as a decimal, and as a percent?

D. Suppose 34 out of 125 sixth-graders surveyed said they would like to try hang gliding. What fraction, decimal, and percent is this?

E. Five out of 73 middle-school students said they look forward to practicing fire drills. What fraction, decimal, and percent is this?

F. 1. Write an explanation for the different strategies you used to express the survey data in percent form.

   2. What general process will cover all of the cases?

ACE Homework starts on page 61.

Did You Know?

Percents, fractions, and decimals are ways to represent ratios. A **ratio** is a comparison of two quantities. If you survey 200 people and report that $\frac{3}{5}$, 0.6, or 60% of the people have driver's licenses, you are comparing the number of people with licenses (120) to the total number of people you asked (200). A phrase such as "120 out of 200" is another way to represent a ratio.

4.4 Changing Forms

There are many different ways to talk about number relationships. When you are telling a story with data, you have choices about how you express the relationships. Fractions or decimals or percents may be more suitable in certain situations.

A survey asked a group of cat owners this question:

During the first year that you owned your cat, how much did it cost?

The table shows how the cat owners responded.

The First-Year Cost of Cat Ownership

Cost	Percent	Decimal	Fraction
$600 and up	▧	0.11	▧
From $500 to $599	25%	▧	▧
From $400 to $499	▧	▧	$\frac{2}{5}$
From $300 to $399	18%	▧	▧
From $200 to $299	▧	▧	$\frac{1}{25}$
Under $200	▧	0.02	▧

Problem 4.4 Moving Between Representations

A. Copy the table above and fill in the missing information.

B. 1. Starting at 0%, shade in different parts of a single percent bar like the one below. Use different colors or shading styles to show the percent corresponding to each of the six choices.

0%   100%

2. Add a key to your percent bar to show what each color or type of shading represents. When you finish, the percent bar should be completely shaded. Explain why.

C. 1. What percent of cat owners had less than $400 in first-year costs?

2. What percent of cat owners had less than $600 in first-year costs?

D. 1. Write each decimal as a percent.

a. 0.3   **b.** 0.21   **c.** 0.115

d. 0.2375   **e.** 2.37

2. Write each percent as a decimal.

a. 17%   **b.** 17.5%

c. 132%   **d.** 132.5%

E. If you were asked to write a story about the first-year costs of cat ownership, would you use data expressed as percents, as fractions, or as decimals? Explain why you think your choice is best.

ACE Homework starts on page 61.

Applications

1. In a recent year, Karl Malone made 474 out of 621 free-throw attempts and John Stockton made 237 out of 287 free-throw attempts. Copy the percent bars and use them to answer each question.

    0   621

    | KARL MALONE |
    0%   100%

    0   287

    | JOHN STOCKTON |
    0%   100%

    a. What fraction benchmark is near the fraction of free throws made by each player?

    b. Estimate the percent of free throws made by each player.

2. Use the data at the right. Which neighborhood (Elmhurst or Little Neck) is more in favor of the proposed school bond to build a new sports complex? Explain your reasoning.

    People Favorable to School Bond

Neighborhood	Yes	No
Elmhurst	43	57
Little Neck	41	9

3. **Multiple Choice** Choose the best score on a quiz.

    A. 15 points out of 25   **B.** 8 points out of 14

    C. 25 points out of 45   **D.** 27 points out of 50

4. **Multiple Choice** Choose the best score on a quiz.

    F. 150 points out of 250   **G.** 24 points out of 42

    H. 75 points out of 135   **J.** 75 points out of 150

5. **Multiple Choice** What is the percent correct for a quiz score of 14 points out of 20?

    A. 43%   **B.** 53%   **C.** 70%   **D.** 75%

Homework Help nline
PHSchool.com
For: Help with Exercise 5
Web Code: ame-2405

6. **Multiple Choice** What is the percent correct for a quiz score of 26 points out of 60?

    F. about 43%   **G.** about 57%   **H.** about 68%   **J.** about 76%

For Exercises 7–15, use the cat data in the table.

Weight (lb.)	Males		Females	
	Kitten	Adult	Kitten	Adult
0–5.9	8	1	7	4
6–10.9	0	16	0	31
11–15.9	2	15	0	10
16–20	0	4	0	2
Total	10	36	7	47

Distribution of Cat Weights

7. **a.** What fraction of the cats are female?

  b. What fraction of the cats are male?

  c. Write each fraction as a decimal and as a percent.

8. **a.** What fraction of the cats are kittens?

  b. What fraction of the cats are adults?

  c. Write each fraction as a decimal and a percent.

9. **a.** What fraction of the kittens are male?

  b. Write the fraction as a decimal and as a percent.

10. What percent of the cats weigh from 11 to 15.9 pounds?

11. What percent of the cats weigh from 0 to 5.9 pounds?

12. What percent of the cats are male kittens and weigh from 11 to 15.9 pounds?

13. What percent of the cats are female and weigh from 6 to 15.9 pounds?

14. What percent of the cats are kittens and weigh from 16 to 20 pounds?

15. What percent of the females weigh from 0 to 5.9 pounds?

In a recent survey, 150 dog owners and 200 cat owners were asked what type of food their pets liked. Here are the results of the survey.

Pet Food Preferences

Preference	Out of 150 Dog Owners	Out of 200 Cat Owners
Human Food Only	75	36
Pet Food Only	45	116
Human and Pet Food	30	48

16. Find the food category that the greatest number of dog owners say is favored by their pets. Write the number in this category as a fraction, as a decimal, and as a percent of the total dog owners surveyed.

17. Find the food category that the greatest number of cat owners say is favored by their pets. Write the number in this category as a fraction, as a decimal, and as a percent of the total cat owners surveyed.

18. Suppose only 100 dog owners were surveyed, with similar results. Estimate how many would have answered in each of the three categories.

19. Suppose 50 cat owners were surveyed, with similar results. Estimate how many would have answered in each of the three categories.

20. Elisa's math test score, with extra credit included, was $\frac{26}{25}$. What percent is this?

21. Suppose 12% of students surveyed said they have tried rock climbing. Estimate how many would say they have tried rock climbing if

    a. 100 students were surveyed

    b. 200 students were surveyed

    c. 150 students were surveyed

22. When surveyed, 78% of pet owners said they live in a town where there is a pooper-scooper law in effect.

  a. How would you express this percent as a decimal?

  b. How would you express this percent as a fraction?

  c. What percent of people surveyed said they do not live in a town with a pooper-scooper law? Explain your reasoning. Express this percent as a decimal and as a fraction.

  d. Can you determine how many people were surveyed? Why or why not?

23. When surveyed, 66% of dog owners who took their dog to obedience school said their dog passed.

  a. What percent of the dog owners said their dogs did not pass?

  b. Write an explanation for a friend about how to solve part (a) and why your solution works.

24. Copy the table below and fill in the missing parts.

Percent	Decimal	Fraction
62%	▓	▓
▓	▓	$\frac{4}{9}$
▓	1.23	▓
▓	▓	$\frac{12}{15}$
▓	2.65	▓
▓	0.55	▓
48%	▓	▓
▓	▓	$\frac{12}{10}$

Go Online
PHSchool.com

For: Multiple-Choice Skills
Practice
Web Code: ama-2454

25. When Diane and Marla got their partner quiz back, their grade was 105% because they got some of the extra credit problems correct.

  a. Write this percent as a decimal and as a fraction.

  b. If each problem on the test had the same point value, how many problems could have been on the test?

Connections

Compare each pair of fractions in Exercises 26–31 using benchmarks or another strategy that makes sense to you. Copy the fractions and insert $<$, $>$, or $=$ to make a true statement.

26. $\dfrac{7}{10}$ ■ $\dfrac{5}{8}$

27. $\dfrac{11}{12}$ ■ $\dfrac{12}{13}$

28. $\dfrac{12}{15}$ ■ $\dfrac{12}{14}$

29. $\dfrac{3}{8}$ ■ $\dfrac{4}{8}$

30. $\dfrac{3}{5}$ ■ $\dfrac{4}{6}$

31. $\dfrac{4}{3}$ ■ $\dfrac{15}{12}$

32. Copy the table below and fill in the missing parts.

Fraction	Mixed Number
$\dfrac{13}{5}$	■
■	$5\dfrac{2}{7}$
■	$9\dfrac{3}{4}$
$\dfrac{23}{3}$	■

33. The following percents are a good set of benchmarks to know because they have nice fraction equivalents and some nice decimal equivalents. Copy the table and fill in the missing parts. Use your table until you have learned these relationships.

Percent	10%	$12\dfrac{1}{2}\%$	20%	25%	30%	$33\dfrac{1}{3}\%$	50%	$66\dfrac{2}{3}\%$	75%
Fraction	■	■	■	■	■	■	■	■	■
Decimal	■	■	■	■	■	■	■	■	■

Extensions

In Exercises 34–36, determine what fraction is the correct label for the mark halfway between the two marked values on the number line. Then write the fraction as a percent and as a decimal.

34.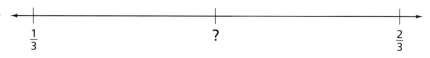
$\frac{1}{3}$? $\frac{2}{3}$

35.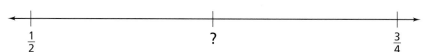
$\frac{1}{2}$? $\frac{3}{4}$

36.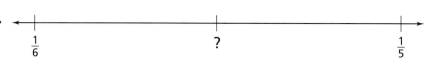
$\frac{1}{6}$? $\frac{1}{5}$

37. What fraction of the square below is shaded? Explain your reasoning.

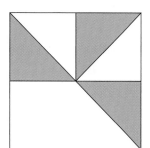

38. In decimal form, what part of the square below is shaded? Explain.

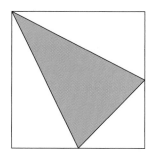

39. What percent of the square below is shaded? Explain.

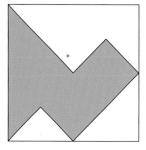

40. A pet store sells digestible mouthwash for cats. To promote the new product, the store is offering $0.50 off the regular price of $2.00 for an 8-ounce bottle. What is the percent discount on the mouthwash?

In Exercises 41–43, determine what number is the correct label for the place halfway between the two percents marked on the percent bar. Then determine what percent the number represents.

41.

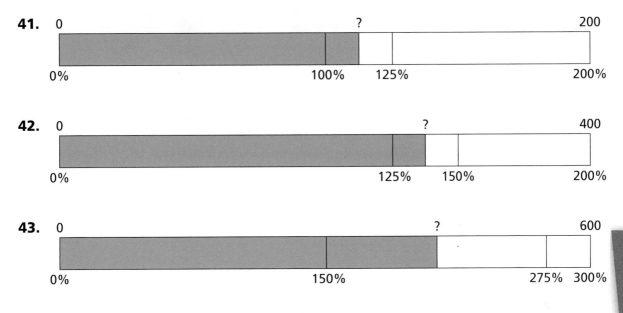

0   ?   200
0%   100% 125%   200%

42.

0   ?   400
0%   125% 150%   200%

43.

0   ?   600
0%   150%   275% 300%

44. A store offers a discount of 30% on all reference books.

   a. If a dictionary costs $12.00 before the discount, what is the amount of the discount?

   b. If a book on insect identification originally costs $15.00, how much will you have to pay for it?

Mathematical Reflections 4

In this investigation, you explored relationships among fractions, decimals, and percents and solved problems using percents to help make comparisons. These questions will help you summarize what you have learned.

Think about your answers to these questions. Discuss your ideas with other students and your teacher. Then write a summary of your findings in your notebook.

1. What does percent mean?

2. **a.** Describe how you can change a percent to a decimal and to a fraction.

   b. Describe how you can change a fraction to a percent.

   c. Describe how you can change a decimal to a percent.

3. Why are percents useful in making comparisons?

4. Explain how to find what percent one number is of another number. For example, what percent of 200 is 75? Draw a percent bar to help explain your thinking.

Looking Back and Looking Ahead

Go Online
PHSchool.com
For: Vocabulary Review
Puzzle
Web code: amj-2051

Working on the problems of this unit extended your knowledge of fractions, decimals, and percents. You learned how

- to relate fractions and decimals to their locations on a number line
- fractions, decimals, and percents are related to each other
- to compare and order fractions and decimals
- to identify equivalent fractions, decimals, and percents

Use Your Understanding: Number Sense

Demonstrate your understanding and skill working with fractions, decimals, and percents by solving the following problems.

1. The diagram shows a puzzle made up of familiar shapes. Find a fraction name and a decimal name for the size of each piece.

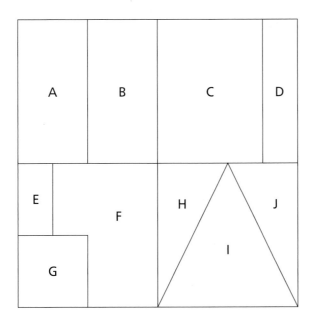

   a. What fraction of the puzzle is covered by each piece? Use your measurement estimation skills and reasoning to find each fraction.

   b. What decimal represents each part of the puzzle?

2. Jose drew eight cards from a deck of number cards. He was asked to show the position of each number on a number line as a fraction, as a decimal, and as a percent of the distance from zero to one.

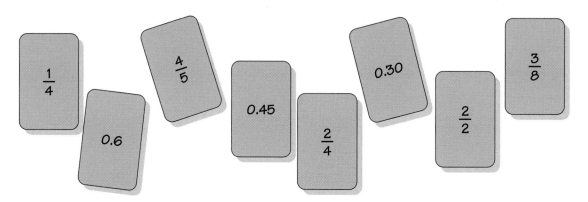

The fraction $\frac{1}{4}$ has already been located on the number line below, along with its corresponding decimal and percent.

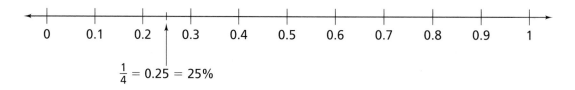

$$\frac{1}{4} = 0.25 = 25\%$$

a. Copy the number line and show the position of each of the other number cards.

b. Label each position as a fraction, a decimal and a percent of the distance from zero to one.

Explain Your Reasoning

You have explored relationships among fractions, decimals, and percents in many different problems. You have learned strategies for working with fractions, decimals, and percents that apply in any situation.

3. Describe a strategy that can be used to compare each pair of numbers.

a. $\frac{5}{8}$ and $\frac{7}{8}$ **b.** $\frac{3}{4}$ and $\frac{3}{5}$ **c.** $\frac{3}{4}$ and $\frac{5}{8}$

d. $\frac{3}{8}$ and $\frac{2}{3}$ **e.** $\frac{3}{4}$ and $\frac{4}{5}$ **f.** $\frac{2}{3}$ and $\frac{5}{8}$

Describe a strategy that can be used to find

4. a fraction equivalent to $\frac{16}{20}$

5. a decimal equivalent to $\frac{16}{20}$

6. a percent for $\frac{16}{20}$

7. a decimal equivalent to 0.18

8. a fraction equivalent to 0.18

9. a percent for 0.18

10. a fraction for 35%

11. a decimal for 3%

Look Ahead

Fractions, decimals, and percents will be used in almost every future unit of *Connected Mathematics.* They are also used in applications of mathematics to problems in science, business, and personal life. You will use them in work on probability, geometry, measurement, and algebra.

In the unit *Bits and Pieces II,* you will learn the operations of addition, subtraction, multiplication, and division of fractions. In *Bits and Pieces III,* you will learn the operations for addition, subtraction, multiplication, and division of decimals and look at additional ways percents are used in the world around us.

B

base ten number system The common number system we use. Our number system is based on the number 10 because we have ten fingers with which to group. Each group represents ten of the previous group, so we can write numbers efficiently. By extending the place value system to include places that represent fractions with 10 or powers of 10 in the denominator, we can easily represent very large and very small quantities. Below is a graphic representation of counting in the base ten number system.

sistema numérico de base diez El sistema numérico que usamos habitualmente. Nuestro sistema numérico está basado en el número 10 porque tenemos diez dedos con los cuales agrupar. Cada grupo representa diez del grupo anterior, así podemos escribir números eficazmente. Si extendemos el sistema de valor posicional para incluir lugares que representen fracciones con 10 o con potencias de 10 en el denominador, podemos representar fácilmente cantidades muy grandes o muy pequeñas. Arriba tienes una representación gráfica de cómo contar con el sistema numérico de base diez.

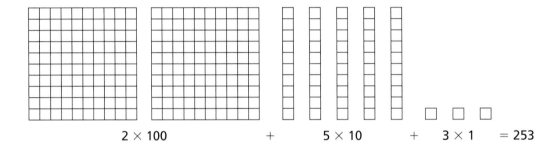

$$2 \times 100 \qquad + \qquad 5 \times 10 \qquad + \qquad 3 \times 1 \qquad = 253$$

benchmark A reference number that can be used to estimate the size of other numbers. For work with fractions, $0, \frac{1}{2}$, and 1 are good benchmarks. We often estimate fractions or decimals with benchmarks because it is easier to do arithmetic with them, and estimates often give enough accuracy for the situation. For example, many fractions and decimals—such as $\frac{37}{50}, \frac{5}{8}, 0.43$, and 0.55—can be thought of as being close to $\frac{1}{2}$. You might say $\frac{5}{8}$ is between $\frac{1}{2}$ and 1 but closer to $\frac{1}{2}$, so you can estimate $\frac{5}{8}$ to be about $\frac{1}{2}$. We also use benchmarks to help compare fractions and decimals. For example, we could say that $\frac{5}{8}$ is greater than 0.43 because $\frac{5}{8}$ is greater than $\frac{1}{2}$ and 0.43 is less than $\frac{1}{2}$.

punto de referencia Un número de comparación que se puede usar para estimar el tamaño de otros números. Para trabajar con fracciones, $0, \frac{1}{2}$ y 1 son buenos puntos de referencia. Por lo general, estimamos fracciones o decimales con puntos de referencia porque nos resulta más fácil hacer cálculos aritméticos con ellos, y las estimaciones suelen ser bastante exactas para la situación. Por ejemplo, muchas fracciones y decimales, como por ejemplo $\frac{37}{50}, \frac{5}{8}, 0.43$ y 0.55, se pueden considerar como cercanas a $\frac{1}{2}$. Se podría decir que $\frac{5}{8}$ está entre $\frac{1}{2}$ y 1, pero más cerca de $\frac{1}{2}$, por lo que se puede estimar que $\frac{5}{8}$ es alrededor de $\frac{1}{2}$ También usamos puntos de referencia para ayudarnos a comparar fracciones y decimales. Por ejemplo, podríamos decir que $\frac{5}{8}$ es mayor que 0.43, porque $\frac{5}{8}$ es mayor que $\frac{1}{2}$ y 0.43 es menor que $\frac{1}{2}$.

decimal A special form of a fraction. Decimals, or decimal fractions, are based on the base ten place-value system. To write numbers as decimals, we use only 10 and powers of 10 as denominators. Writing fractions in this way saves us from writing the denominators because they are understood. When we write $\frac{375}{1,000}$ as a decimal (0.375) the denominator of 1,000 is understood. The digits to the left of the decimal point show whole units. The digits to the right of the decimal point show a portion of a whole unit. The diagram shows the place value for each digit of the number 5,620.301.

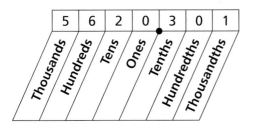

denominator The number written below the line in a fraction. In the fraction $\frac{3}{4}$, 4 is the denominator. In the part-whole interpretation of fractions, the denominator shows the number of equal-size parts into which the whole has been split.

equivalent fractions Fractions that are equal in value, but may have different numerators and denominators. For example, $\frac{2}{3}$ and $\frac{14}{21}$ are equivalent fractions. The shaded part of this rectangle represents both $\frac{2}{3}$ and $\frac{14}{21}$.

decimal Una forma especial de fracción. Los decimales, o fracciones decimales, se basan en el sistema de valor relativo de base 10. Para escribir números como decimales, usamos solamente 10 y potencias de 10 como denominadores. Escribir fracciones de esta manera nos evita tener que escribir los denominadores, porque están implícitos. Cuando escribimos $\frac{375}{1,000}$ como un decimal, 0.375, se entiende que el denominador es 1,000. Los dígitos que se encuentran a la izquierda del punto decimal muestran unidades enteras, y los dígitos a la derecha del punto decimal muestran una porción de una unidad entera. El diagrama muestra el valor relativo para cada dígito del número 5,620.301.

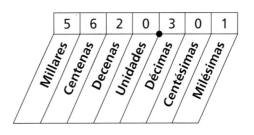

denominador El número escrito debajo de la línea en una fracción. En la fracción $\frac{3}{4}$, 4 es el denominador. En la interpretación de partes y enteros de fracciones, el denominador muestra el número de partes iguales en que fue dividido el entero.

fracciones equivalentes Fracciones de igual valor, pero que pueden tener diferentes numeradores y denominadores. Por ejemplo, $\frac{2}{3}$ y $\frac{14}{21}$ son fracciones equivalentes. La parte sombreada de este rectángulo representa tanto $\frac{2}{3}$ como $\frac{14}{21}$.

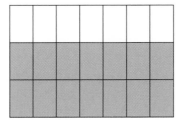

fraction A number (quantity) of the form $\frac{a}{b}$ where a and b are whole numbers. A fraction can indicate a part of a whole object, set, or measurement unit; a ratio of two quantities; or a division. For the picture below, the fraction $\frac{3}{4}$ shows the part of the rectangle that is shaded. The denominator 4 indicates the number of equal-sized pieces. The numerator 3 indicates the number of pieces that are shaded.

fracción Un número (una cantidad) en forma de $\frac{a}{b}$, donde a y b son números enteros. Una fracción puede indicar una parte de un objeto, conjunto de objetos enteros, o unidad de la medida; una razón entre dos cantidades; o una división. Para el dibujo de abajo, la fracción $\frac{3}{4}$ muestra la parte del rectángulo que está sombreada. El denominador 4 indica la cantidad de piezas de igual tamaño. El numerador 3 indica la cantidad de piezas que están sombreadas.

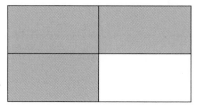

The fraction $\frac{3}{4}$ could also represent three of a group of four items meeting a particular criteria. For example, when 12 students enjoyed a particular activity and 16 students did not, the ratio is 3 to 4. Another example is the amount of pizza each person receives when three pizzas are shared equally among four people ($3 \div 4$ or $\frac{3}{4}$ of a pizza per person).

La fracción $\frac{3}{4}$ también podría representar 3 en un grupo de cuatro elementos que cumplan con un mismo criterio. Por ejemplo, cuando 12 estudiantes participaron en una determinada actividad y 16 estudiantes no lo hicieron, la razón es 3 a 4. Otro ejemplo es la cantidad de pizza que le toca a cada persona cuando se reparten tres pizzas en partes iguales entre cuatro personas ($3 \div 4$ ó $\frac{3}{4}$ de pizza por persona).

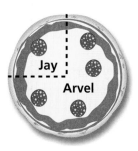  

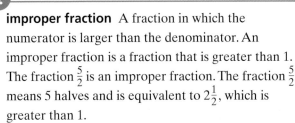

I

improper fraction A fraction in which the numerator is larger than the denominator. An improper fraction is a fraction that is greater than 1. The fraction $\frac{5}{2}$ is an improper fraction. The fraction $\frac{5}{2}$ means 5 halves and is equivalent to $2\frac{1}{2}$, which is greater than 1.

fracción impropia Una fracción cuyo numerador es mayor que el denominador. Una fracción impropia es una fracción mayor que 1. La fracción $\frac{5}{2}$ es una fracción impropia. La fracción $\frac{5}{2}$ representa 5 mitades y es equivalente a $2\frac{1}{2}$, lo cual es mayor que 1.

M

mixed number A number that is written with both a whole number and a fraction. A mixed number is the sum of the whole number and the fraction. The number $2\frac{1}{2}$ represents two wholes and one half and can be thought of as $2 + \frac{1}{2}$.

número mixto Un número que se escribe con un número entero y una fracción. Un número mixto es la suma del número entero y la fracción. El número $2\frac{1}{2}$ representa dos enteros y un medio, y se puede considerar como $2 + \frac{1}{2}$.

N

numerator The number written above the line in a fraction. In the fraction $\frac{5}{8}$, 5 is the numerator. When you interpret the fraction $\frac{5}{8}$ as a part of a whole, the numerator represents 5 of 8 equal parts.

numerador El número escrito sobre la línea en una fracción. En la fracción $\frac{5}{8}$, 5 es el numerador. Cuando interpretas la fracción $\frac{5}{8}$ como parte de un entero, el numerador representa 5 de 8 partes iguales.

P

percent "Out of 100." A percent is a special decimal fraction in which the denominator is 100. When we write 68%, we mean 68 out of 100, $\frac{68}{100}$, or 0.68. We write the percent sign (%) after a number to indicate percent. The shaded part of this square is 68%.

porcentaje "La parte de 100". Un porcentaje es una fracción decimal especial en la que el denominador es 100. Cuando escribimos 68%, queremos decir 68 de 100, $\frac{68}{100}$ ó 0.68. Para indicar porcentaje escribimos el signo correspondiente (%) después del número. La parte sombreada de este cuadrado es 68%.

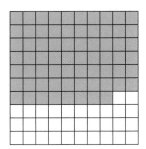

R

ratio A number, often expressed as a fraction, used to make comparisons between two quantities. Ratios may also be expressed as equivalent decimals or percents. $\frac{3}{5}$, 0.6, and 60% are all ratios. A phrase such as "120 out of 200" is another way to represent a ratio. Here are three ways to show the same ratio:

$$\frac{3}{5} \qquad 3 \text{ to } 5 \qquad 3 : 5$$

razón Un número, a menudo expresado como fracción, que se usa para hacer comparaciones entre dos cantidades. Las razones también se pueden expresar como decimales equivalentes o porcentajes. $\frac{3}{5}$, 0.6, y 60% también son razones. Una frase como "120 de 200" es otra forma de representar una razón. Aquí están tres maneras de demostrar la misma razón:

$$\frac{3}{5} \qquad 3 \text{ a } 5 \qquad 3 : 5$$

rational number A number that can be written as a quotient of two positive or negative numbers. You are familiar with positive rational numbers like $\frac{3}{4}$, $\frac{107}{5}$, and $3\left(\frac{3}{1}\right)$. Some examples of the negative rational numbers you will see in the future are $^{-}3$, $\frac{-2}{5}$, and $^{-}20$. Both positive and negative rational numbers can be used to represent real-life situations. For example, temperatures or yardage during a football game can be positive, negative, or 0. There are other numbers, such as pi, that are *not* rational numbers.

número racional Número que se puede expresar como cociente de dos números enteros positivos o negativos. Tú ya conoces los números racionales positivos, como $\frac{3}{4}$, $\frac{107}{5}$, y $3\left(\frac{3}{1}\right)$. Algunos ejemplos de números racionales negativos que verás en el futuro son $^{-}3$, $\frac{-2}{5}$, y $^{-}20$. Tanto los números racionales positivos como negativos se pueden usar para representar situaciones de la vida real. Por ejemplo, las temperaturas o las medidas en yardas en un partido de fútbol americano pueden ser positivas, negativas o 0. Hay otros números, como pi, que no son números racionales.

U

unit fraction A fraction with a numerator of 1. In the unit fraction $\frac{1}{13}$, the denominator 13 indicates the number of equal-size parts into which the whole has been split. The fraction represents the quantity of one of those parts.

fracción de unidad Una fracción con numerador 1. En la fracción de unidad $\frac{1}{13}$, el denominador 13 indica la cantidad de partes iguales en las que se ha dividido el entero, y que la fracción representa uno de esas partes.

Academic Vocabulary

Academic vocabulary words are words that you see in textbooks and on tests. These are not math vocabulary terms, but knowing them will help you succeed in mathematics.

Las palabras de vocabulario académico son palabras que ves en los libros de texto y en las pruebas. Éstos no son términos de vocabulario de matemáticas, pero conocerlos te ayudará a tener éxito en matemáticas.

C

compare To tell or show how two things are alike and different.
related terms: analyze, relate

Sample: Compare the fractions $\frac{2}{3}$ and $\frac{3}{8}$.

comparar Decir o mostrar en qué se parecen y en qué son diferentes dos cosas.
términos relacionados: analizar, relacionar

Ejemplo: Compara las fracciones $\frac{2}{3}$ y $\frac{3}{8}$.

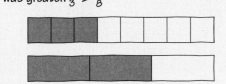

I set the fractions strips representing $\frac{2}{3}$ and $\frac{3}{8}$ next to each other to see which fraction was greater. $\frac{2}{3} > \frac{3}{8}$

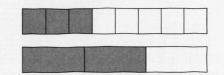

Coloco las tiras de fracciones que representan $\frac{2}{3}$ y $\frac{3}{8}$ una junto a la otra para ver cuál fracción es mayor. $\frac{2}{3} > \frac{3}{8}$

D

describe To explain or tell in detail. A written description can contain facts and other information needed to communicate your answer. A diagram or a graph may also be included.
related terms: express, explain, illustrate

Sample: Describe in writing or with pictures how $\frac{5}{4}$ compares to $1\frac{1}{4}$.

describir Explicar o decir con detalle. Una descripción escrita puede contener hechos y otra información necesaria para comunicar tu respuesta. También se puede incluir un diagrama o una gráfica.
términos relacionados: expresar, explicar, ilustrar

Ejemplo: Describe por escrito o con imágenes cómo $\frac{5}{4}$ se compara con $1\frac{1}{4}$.

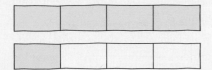

I can use fraction strips divided into fourths to show that $1\frac{1}{4}$ is equal to $\frac{5}{4}$.

I can also compare using division. 5 divided by 4 is 1 remainder 1. So $\frac{5}{4}$ is the same as $1\frac{1}{4}$.

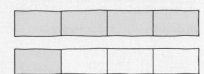

Puedo usar tiras de fracciones divididas en cuartos para mostrar que $1\frac{1}{4}$ es igual a $\frac{5}{4}$.

También puedo comparar usando la división. 5 dividido entre 4 es 1 con un residuo de 1. Así, $\frac{5}{4}$ es lo mismo que $1\frac{1}{4}$.

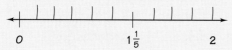

estimate To find an approximate answer that is relatively close to an exact amount.

related terms: approximate, guess

Sample: Estimate and mark where the number 2 should be on the number line below. Explain.

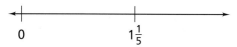

0	$1\frac{1}{5}$

Since $1\frac{1}{5}$ is the same as $\frac{6}{5}$, I divided the space between 0 and $1\frac{1}{5}$ into six parts. This gives me an idea of the length of $\frac{1}{5}$.

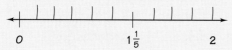

| 0 | | $1\frac{1}{5}$ | | 2 |

Then I added 4 marks after $1\frac{1}{5}$ to estimate where $1\frac{5}{5}$, or 2, should be on the number line.

estimar Hallar una respuesta aproximada que esté relativamente cerca de una cantidad exacta.

términos relacionados: aproximar, conjeturar

Ejemplo: Estima y marca dónde debería estar el número 2 en la recta numérica que sigue. Explica tu respuesta.

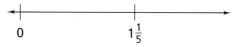

0	$1\frac{1}{5}$

Puesto que $1\frac{1}{5}$ es lo mismo que $\frac{6}{5}$, divido el espacio entre 0 y $1\frac{1}{5}$ en cinco partes. Esto me da una idea de la longitud de $\frac{1}{5}$.

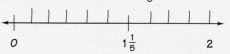

| 0 | | $1\frac{1}{5}$ | | 2 |

Luego agrego 4 marcas después de $1\frac{1}{5}$ para estimar donde debería estar $1\frac{5}{5}$, ó 2, en la recta numérica.

---

explain To give facts and details that make an idea easier to understand. Explaining can involve a written summary supported by a diagram, chart, table, or a combination of these.

related terms: analyze, clarify, describe, justify, tell

Sample: Explain why $\frac{9}{10}$ is greater than $\frac{7}{8}$.

I can write the fractions in decimal form and compare digits.

$\frac{9}{10}$	0.900
$\frac{7}{8}$	0.875

Because 9 in the tenths place is greater than 8, $\frac{9}{10}$ is greater than $\frac{7}{8}$.

I can also write equivalent fractions with a common denominator and compare the numerators. Since $\frac{9}{10}$ is equivalent to $\frac{36}{40}$ and $\frac{7}{8}$ is equivalent to $\frac{35}{40}$, and 36 is greater than 35, $\frac{9}{10}$ is greater than $\frac{7}{8}$.

explicar Dar hechos y detalles que hacen que una idea sea más fácil de comprender. Explicar puede implicar un resumen escrito apoyado por hechos, un diagrama, una gráfica, una tabla o una combinación de éstos.

términos relacionados: analizar, aclarar, describir, justificar, decir

Ejemplo: Explica por qué $\frac{9}{10}$ es mayor que $\frac{7}{8}$.

Puedo escribir las fracciones en forma decimal y comparar los dígitos.

$\frac{9}{10}$	0.900
$\frac{7}{8}$	0.875

Puesto que 9 en el lugar de los décimos es mayor que 8, $\frac{9}{10}$ es mayor que $\frac{7}{8}$.

También puedo escribir fracciones equivalentes con un común denominador y comparar los numeradores. Puesto que $\frac{9}{10}$ es equivalente a $\frac{36}{40}$ y $\frac{7}{8}$ es equivalente a $\frac{35}{40}$ y 36 es mayor que 35, $\frac{9}{10}$ es mayor que $\frac{7}{8}$.

Index

Acknowledgments

Team Credits

The people who made up the **Connected Mathematics2** team—representing editorial, editorial services, design services, and production services—are listed below. Bold type denotes core team members.

Leora Adler, Judith Buice, Kerry Cashman, Patrick Culleton, Sheila DeFazio, Richard Heater, **Barbara Hollingdale, Jayne Holman,** Karen Holtzman, **Etta Jacobs,** Christine Lee, Carolyn Lock, Cathie Maglio, **Dotti Marshall,** Rich McMahon, Eve Melnechuk, Kristin Mingrone, Terri Mitchell, **Marsha Novak,** Irene Rubin, Donna Russo, Robin Samper, Siri Schwartzman, **Nancy Smith,** Emily Soltanoff, **Mark Tricca,** Paula Vergith, Roberta Warshaw, Helen Young

Additional Credits

Diana Bonfilio, Mairead Reddin, Michael Torocsik

Illustration

Michelle Barbera: 8, 14

Technical Illustration

WestWords, Inc.

Cover Design

9 Surf Studios

Photos

2 t, Peter Beck/Corbis; **2 b,** Dave King/Dorling Kindersley; **3 t,** NASA; **3 b,** Eastcott Momatiuk/Getty Images, Inc.; **5,** Richard Haynes; **6,** Richard Haynes; **16,** Colin Keates/Dorling Kindersley; **19,** Tom Stewart/Corbis; **20,** Richard Haynes; **25,** Richard Haynes; **26 both,** Richard Haynes; **28,** Russ Lappa; **35 all,** Russ Lappa; **41,** Richard Haynes; **43,** AP/Wide World Photos/ J. Pat Carter; **44,** Richard Haynes; **49,** Peter Beck/Corbis; **51,** SW Production/Index Stock Imagery, Inc.; **52,** Richard Haynes; **55,** Rocky Widner/NBAE/Getty Images, Inc.; **58,** Dave King/Dorling Kindersley; **61,** Ron Kimball Stock; **63,** Don Mason/Corbis; **64,** Frank Siteman/Getty Images, Inc.; **67,** Russ Lappa

Note: Every effort has been made to locate the copyright owner of the material reprinted in this book. Omissions brought to our attention will be corrected in subsequent editions.